A Meissen porcelain figure of a small child dancing with a lady doll. At that time (c.1850) most dolls were lady dolls.

When the voices of children are heard on the green,
And laughing is heard on the hill,
My heart is at rest within my breast,
Any everything else is still.
    From *Songs of Innocence*, by William Blake (1789).

This book is dedicated to our great-grandchildren, Leslie Marie Carr, Joseph Robert Carr and Noel Thomas Malcolm-Hadley, and to children of all ages.

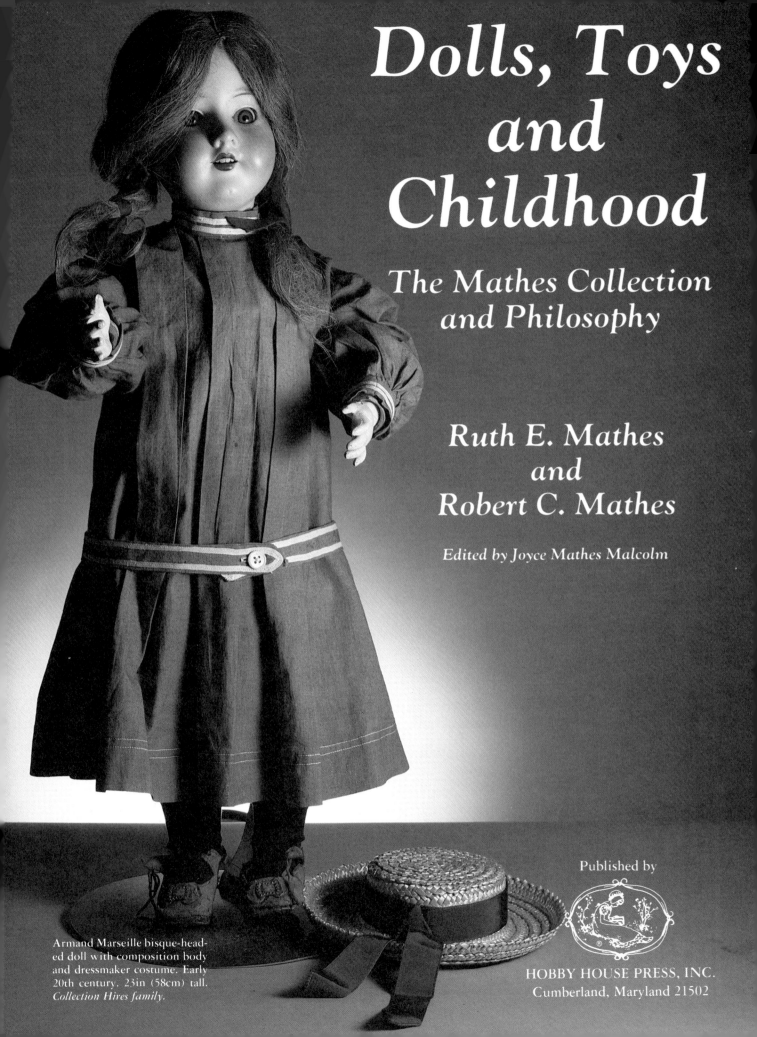

Dolls, Toys and Childhood

The Mathes Collection and Philosophy

Ruth E. Mathes
and
Robert C. Mathes

Edited by Joyce Mathes Malcolm

Armand Marseille bisque-headed doll with composition body
and dressmaker costume. Early
20th century. 23in (58cm) tall.
Collection Hires family.

Published by

HOBBY HOUSE PRESS, INC.
Cumberland, Maryland 21502

Additional Copies of this Book may be Purchased at $19.95
from
Hobby House Press, Inc.
900 Frederick Street
Cumberland, Maryland 21502
or from your favorite bookstore or dealer.
Please add $1.75 per copy for postage.

Printed in the United States of America
ISBN: 0-87588-300-1

Acknowledgments

We can think of no other interest that leads us into so many rewarding fields of enjoyment as the study of dolls. Some of these are history, the church, the child, fashion, folk art, and so on. Best of all, perhaps, are the people we meet and the friendships developed over the years. It breaks down all barriers. These friendships stimulated us to travel, study and open our minds to new horizons. Our list of acknowledgements include collectors, dealers, scholars, writers and museum staff members: Imogene Anderson; Mrs. Edgar Hires; Mary Black; The Doll Collectors of America; Mrs. Earle E. Andrews; Clara Fawcett; Helen Hinckley; Mrs. R. C. Williams (Darcy); Madame de Galea, of France; Alice K. Early, of England; George Ertell; Malcolm Watkins; Flora Gill Jacobs; Walter Laemmle; A. K. Kunze-Lange, of Germany; Sister Corita Kent; Margaret Martin - church dolls; Bea d'Armond; Bart Anderson; Herbert M. Hosmer; Roger Warner, of England; June Douglas; Carl Fox; Bert Solman - English dealer; Mary Hillier, of England; Dorothy S. Coleman; Frank and Theresa Caplan; Philip Morrison; and, Lillian Smith.

Our special thanks go to John Darcy Noble, a social historian, museum curator, artist and expert on toys and dolls. He suggested that we write this book in the first place, and gave us invaluable help in seeing this project through.

Table of Contents

OPPOSITE PAGE: Two pre-Greiner dolls. Papier-mâché heads, cloth bodies, leather arms, and wearing homemade clothes. Emily (left) is 33in (84cm) tall. Abbygail (right) is 35in (89cm) tall.

Patented Greiner dolls with papier-mâché heads. Hair style on the smaller doll is of an earlier period although dated the same as the larger doll. Cloth bodies with leather arms. America. 1858. 32in (81cm) and 21in (53cm) tall.

Foreword

Ruth and Bob Mathes are pioneers, and I have always loved pioneers: brave, vigorous, vital people, endlessly inquiring, full of the joy of the quest and the satisfaction of discovery.

I have the greatest respect for the Mathes, and my respect is enriched by the sharing of the same passionate interests, and reinforced with love and friendship that has been tempered and tested over a quarter of a century. For me, the Mathes are very special people indeed.

Their interest in dolls began as early as the first World War, when they found a postcard of the doll "Letitia Penn" at the Smithsonian Institution, and this interest was sustained by the needs of their two children who were born a few years later.

It was not until the Second World War that they met Imogene Anderson, whose collection was already legendary, and saw Letitia Penn face to face. Mrs. Anderson's encouragement fanned their enthusiasm, and they were "off and running as serious doll collectors."

These were early days, when good old dolls could still be found in trunks and attics, largely ignored by antique dealers. Little was known about them.

The Mathes began their search for dolls, which gathered impetus on their trip to Europe, in 1951. There they made connections, met fascinating people, and found sources of information that have long since disappeared.

Their recollections of these early years must fill today's collectors with envy. Although they write, in 1951, of "dolls becoming much in demand," the field was then open, and good old dolls both plentiful and affordable, on a scale inconceivable today, when old dolls have moved from the "Hobby Shop" category to take their place in the great auction houses, beside paintings and porcelains and other pedigreed antiques.

For their inquiring minds, the dolls they found initiated research, the bases of much of their later work, research conducted always with clear-sightedness and scholarly detachment.

They were — and are still, I believe — unique among doll collectors, in that their approach has always been through the child rather than through the doll as an isolated — and thus distorted — objective. Their article "Research as Applied to Dolls," written in 1973, was in my opinion a milestone.

Their interest began, as I have said, with their own children, which is, of course, the sane, logical approach to the study of toys. Their consuming interest in the playthings of the past is reflected in their concern, not only for the needs of today's children, but for this need as it is multiplied by those children of other cultures, throughout the world. For them, doll collecting was always in the service of enlightenment, of humanitarianism.

But if what the Mathes discovered and made available to others through their lectures and publications was revolutionary in its time, today it is pertinent and more important than ever.

As technology changes our lifestyles and destroys the cultures of small nations around the world, it becomes more and more urgent that we, the privileged, make every effort to understand, respect and protect them.

By doing so, perhaps we can, before it is too late, preserve the priceless heritage of their children, as well as our own. This could be achieved, of course, on many levels. The Mathes, by choosing toys, and especially dolls, as their special field, have gone straight to the heart of cultural survival, the child.

In this book we follow their progress through the years, in their quest for examples to illustrate or confirm their theories. We share with them the excitement of discovery, the joy of research, the exhilaration of encounters with kindred spirits and, eventually, we have the privilege of reviewing their findings.

For me, it is a great satisfaction to see this archive gathered together, safely, between the covers of a book, and illustrated, so beautifully with treasures from the Mathes' rarified collection.

And it is with the utmost pleasure and pride that I introduce to you Ruth and Bob Mathes, now both in their nineties. Japan, that ultimately civilized country, watches over its great men and women in the arts. It not only reveres them, but elevates the best of them to the status of National Living Treasures. It has long seemed to me that the United States might treat its own gifted citizens with similar reverence.

For those of us who are concerned with the future of our children, Ruth and Bob Mathes are, certainly, National Living Treasures.

— John Darcy Noble

Introduction

More than sixty years ago, Ruth and Bob Mathes became interested in collecting dolls and in studying the importance of dolls and other playthings in the development of children. Through the years they have assembled not only an outstanding collection of dolls but also a unique and valuable record of their visits to many of the other famous early doll collectors such as Imogene Anderson, Mme. de Galea and Jacques d'Allemagne, son of Henri d'Allemagne. Modern collectors may recognize these names but it is a rare privilege to have a first-hand account of these people and their collections made by knowledgeable people who actually saw them.

The detailed descriptions of the Mathes' dolls should delight collectors of antique dolls. Few museums, much less private collections, have as many fine early dolls as are in the Mathes' collection. Their eclectic collection of dolls and religious figures includes the many materials from which these were made: wood, wax, papier-mâché, cloth and, of course, the fine porcelains, both china and bisque. Not only the wide ranging developmental toys and figures themselves but also their original clothes and accessories hold great interest and reflect the discriminating taste of the Mathes.

In their attempt to clarify and elucidate, the distinction between "Fashion Dolls" and "Fashionable Dolls" is discussed with clarity in this book. Here the Mathes fall back not into the doll collector's thinking but rather that to which the play doll was originally directed. Too often the term "Fashion Doll" has been used erroneously by other authors. The quotation from the 1711-12 *Spectator* concerning "Fashion Dolls" is very important not only to collectors of dolls but also to costume historians.

Ruth and Bob Mathes, pioneers in research on antique dolls, have always kept to the highest standards in their research. This is especially evident in their study of wooden dolls. Their research on dolls also includes the function of dolls as a working tool in the cultural development of children. They have explored the fact that "Play is the child's work" as it relates to dolls, as well as the socio-economic and historical importance of dolls.

It has been my privilege to know the Mathes, Ruth and Bob, and their daughter, Joyce, for at least a third of their collecting years. Ours has not been a passive acquaintance but rather in keeping with their personalities a very active association. We have visited many museums together and spent numerous happy hours discussing dolls. Now these pleasures, provided by the Mathes, can be shared with others through this book.

— *Dorothy S. Coleman*, 1985

Prologue

A rapidly growing hobby is that of collecting dolls. Why should there be such a hobby and where does it fit into the scheme of things? These notes are a very brief introduction to provide a little background and perspective. Due to its relative youth it is a hobby which still offers a variety of avenues to explore from which individual initiative may produce constructive results.

Individual collectors will have widely different approaches. Many will start with the sentimental impulse of preserving family heirlooms; some will select them as mementos of celebrities; others will be interested in costuming, either historically or creatively, for which dolls provide convenient mannequins; a few will regard them as a form of miniature sculpture for recording character types; many will use them as guideposts to geography or history; some will collect omnivorously and others may specialize in one narrow field such as tin heads, or Kewpies or Brownie dolls. Whatever the motive the sum total of such activities will eventually develop new relationships in our knowledge of human customs, technology, behavior and history; in short, to improve our appreciation in those fields of study called the humanities.

The doll as a toy is of relatively recent origin although its ancestors are lost in the mists of antiquity. Even today the most primitive peoples do not have the child's doll. For them images of the human form are matters of magic and religion and are the province of the medicine man. Life of the "free and noble savage" was in reality tightly constrained by the necessity of providing food and shelter. Little girls were kept busy minding the littler ones instead of having the vicarious satisfaction of cuddling a dolly.

At some point, however, the taboos broke down; perhaps at first in some partial way as in the case of the kachinas of the Hopi Indians. These represent powerful spirits or tribal heros and yet are given to the children for education and for fun. An interesting case is found among the Chacos Indians of Columbia where a crude stick doll of balsa wood is given to the child when one year old, after a witch doctor has installed a guardian spirit in it by magical rites.

The point at which some images may first be regarded as dolls might reasonably be when toys, in general, appear on the scene. These can be identified as such when arranged to perform some action. Some have been found in prehistoric Egyptian and Greek cultures. When found as human images having moveable arms and legs, these may have been dolls. Such are generally made

Two all original German peg-woodens of the Victorian period, mid 19th century. All original. 11in (28cm) and 10in (25cm) tall.

ABOVE: Papier-mâché head dolls with ornately styled hair, kid bodies and wooden arms and legs. The two dolls in front are all original. Early 19th century. 12in (31cm), 12in (31cm), 11½in (29cm) and 9½in (24cm) tall.

Papier-mâché poupards 19in (48cm), 12in (31cm) and 13½in (34cm) tall. France. 19th century.

Illustration 1: Bone Coptic dolls dating from 500 A.D. depicting a mother and swaddling babe. 3½in (9cm) and 2½in (6cm) tall.

of terra cotta, metal or ivory, but in the most favorable climatic conditions, an occasional cloth or wooden figure survived.

This transition from the sacred image to the child's toy has led some to say that the word "doll" comes from the same Greek root as the word "idol." The fact is much more human. The word is purely English in derivation, being a diminutive or baby-talk shortening of the name Dorothy; just as Hal is of Harry or Moll, of Mary. During the 16th and 17th centuries the word was used as a pet name for a girl friend, while the accepted term for the child's toy was babe or baby, used well into the 18th century. By 1700 "doll" was defined in a dictionary as a child's toy. The selection of Dolly instead of Molly or Betty was probably not happenstance as the Scotch word for doll or puppet is "doroty." Of recent years a retransferal of the word to humans has taken place as in the title of the musical revue *Guys and Dolls.* This occurred in slang at least as far back as 1785, for Grose's *Dictionary of the Vulgar Tongue* defines doll as, "Bartholomew doll, a tawdry overdressed woman like one of the children's dolls sold at Bartholomew Fair."

It seems fair to say that dolls, at least as the product of craftsmen, appeared along with leisure. Only the nobles and the wealthy could afford them. They were made of the same materials as sacred images — terra cotta, stone, bronze, wax, ivory, bone and wood. If the lower classes tried to emulate their betters, it was probably in dried clay, straw, twigs and rags. These lesser images have, of course, not been preserved.

Surviving examples of sacred and secular figures from the early Egyptian, Greek and Roman cultures are for the most part crude. The Dark Ages in turn seemed to have blotted out dolls along with other amenities of good living. With the Renaissance there was a resurgence of fine craftsmanship applied to all kinds of figures — church images, decorative figurines, fashion mannequins, artists models and finally, dolls for the wealthy. An important point is that the making of such items was under the control of the craft guilds, so that carving was done by one guild, painting by another, costuming by still another. Thus early dolls partook of the nature of folk art. This continued well into the 18th century and, for some types of dolls produced as a home craft, well into the 19th.

One of the intriguing features of the doll hobby is to correlate the social and technological changes with the kinds and qualities of the dolls of the time. This in turn is of value in classifying and dating specimens. To illustrate this we will discuss later, in some detail, these factors for the early wooden dolls of the crafts period. Similar

Illustration 2: Greek clay figure with separated head. Pre-Christian era. Note hole through shoulders for arm attachment. 4in (10cm) tall.

treatment for the multitude of more modern dolls would be too lengthy for this prologue. Wood was the most popular early material for sacred and secular images. It is easily shaped and finished, plentiful and not fragile. In spite of its somewhat perishable nature, most specimens available for collectors from around the 18th century are of wood.

The skills developed in making church images was ready at hand for the doll maker, but rather more so on the Continent than in England where the making of images had become anathema under Cromwell. Thus, on the whole, more finely carved dolls were made on the Continent. The effect of social change is most striking in England.

At the end of the 17th century a doll was being made with the head and body in one solid block of wood, hence often called the blockhead doll. Only the face was naturalistically carved and finished, coated with gesso and enamelled with varnish. The sculptured eyes were painted. Arms and legs were usually very crude. Next, some were made with flat porcelain or glass eyes having large black pupils and no iris. These two types are often called Queen Anne dolls and later ones Queen Anne-type. A better term is English woodens which covers the whole period of these English dolls, the 18th century, plus and minus a few decades.

England's prosperity was now developing a large middle class providing a new market for moderate priced articles, including dolls. With the full impact of the Industrial Revolution, about mid 18th century, mass production methods ensued. Blocks of wood, hastily turned on a lathe, came out bodies with heads, shoulders and hips, all the same diameter. The nearly spherical heads had almost no carving for the features. Smaller eyes, set close together, gave them a cross-eyed look and the painting of the face became highly conventionalized. About the year 1800 the last extreme steps in cheapening were taken; all carving was eliminated by molding on a face of plaster and the glass eyes replaced by the briefest indication in paint. Even so, they were unable to meet the competition of a new form of wooden doll from the Tyrol area of Europe, and the commercial making of wooden dolls in England finally came to an end.

The creation of this new form of doll from the Tyrol was stimulated by the reduction in demand for sacred images from the northern part of Europe following the Reformation. This challenge was met by the wood-carvers of the Grödner Tal (then in Austria, now the Val Gardena in Italy) who combined the facility in carving charming little faces with the very ingenious jointing system, used for centuries past in *artist's models*. These "peg-woodens" were made in stock sizes from one-half inch to two feet (1cm to 61cm). They took over the market in England where they were called "penny woodens" or "Dutch dolls" (Dutch from Deutsch, as they were wholesaled through Nuremberg, Germany). They were pretty, low in cost, and adjustable to almost any posture. Even Princess Victoria dressed 32 herself and

Illustration 3: Two artists' models made at the time of the carving of church figures. Germany. 18th century. 25in (64cm) and 15in (38cm) tall.

they were used for dolls' houses and hobbies all through the 19th century.

The impact of change came even more rapidly with the beginning of the 19th century. Wholesale firms, dealing only in toys, became established in Nuremberg, soon making it the toy center of the world. Their activities increased the economic competition between different techniques for making toys. Quantity production made molding processes very important. Nice heads could be made much cheaper by molding in plaster, china, wax or papier-mâché than by carving. Some of these molded heads were put on peg-wooden bodies (referred to by us as "alien heads"), still others on stuffed kid or cloth bodies. The effect on the all woodens was devastating. The Tyrolean peasants were forced into cheapening their product. By 1850 the peg-woodens were being so crudely made that many have thought them to be a more primitive form from the 18th century; even experienced collectors and museums thought so. Yet they were so cheap and still so popular with the children and for hobbies that in 1875 shipments to England from the Grödner Tal ran as high as several tons per week.

China head doll with homemade body and clothes wearing child's shoes. Germany. 1880s. 27in (69cm) tall. Small china head doll in cradle has cloth body and china arms and legs. Wearing homemade clothing. Early 20th century. 13in (33cm) tall.

ABOVE: Two wax-over papier-mâché head dolls found in Scotland. Original clothing. Wire pull eyes. Large doll is 29in (74cm) tall; smaller doll is 13in (33cm) tall. Germany. Early 19th century.

Poured wax doll with wax arms and legs on a cloth body. Needle inserted hair and eyebrows. Original clothing. England. 1880s. 24in (61cm) tall.

Illustration 4. Group of seven peg-wooden dolls with china (alien) heads. Germany. 19th century. 5in (13cm) to 5½in (19cm) tall.

Indeed, this is a trend to look for generally; a given type of doll may appear first as a quality product and then be cheapened as a wider market develops. In the case of glazed china doll heads some of the earliest (possibly more correctly regarded as figurines) were made in the latter part of the 18th century of the finest porcelain. In the early part of the 19th century the development of the ceramic heads moved rapidly into a wide range of qualities — fancy Dresdens after 1840, translucent rosy glazes, parians after 1860 and so on down to bisque and crude stoneware.

In turn the glazed china lost out in popularity to the bisque or unglazed porcelain which supplied a more realistic complexion. While most chinas had molded hair, fixed heads and painted eyes, the bisques offered new attractions — hair wigs, pivot heads and blown glass eyes, both fixed and sleeping type. A few of the finer chinas also tried these latter attractions but the bisques took the lead. Although Germany was the great mass producer of both types, the French took up the production of the luxury grade bisque doll. For this reason the finest bisque, although also made in Germany, is called French bisque. The French made dolls with especially nice features, pivot heads, jointed bodies of many types and featured elaborate dressing in the latest fashion. Jumeau and Bru were the leaders in making this class of doll which have come to be known erroneously among collectors as "French Fashion Dolls."

This is an unfortunate term as it has led to the myth that they were designed for the purpose of sending the latest French fashions around the world. It is true that dolls (or mannequins similar to dolls) were at one time used for this purpose for some four or five centuries before the appearance of the colored fashion plate. They alone deserve to be called "fashion dolls," and the need for them disappeared by 1800. Possibly an occasional doll was dressed to show a fashion and sent to this country up to 1830 when *Godey's Lady's Book* appeared. The fine French bisque, in its heyday from 1860 to 1890, was made and sold as a luxury toy for girls.

The process of molding various "pulps" to make doll faces was practiced in Nuremberg in 1700. Quantity production began around 1800, using papier-mâché. In one early form coated with wax, the round-faced heads bear such a striking resemblance to the late Queen Anne-type, that one suspects one of those wooden doll heads to have been the model on which the molds were cast. These also used the same "simple eye" which appear in the mid 18th century English woodens. More natural featured wax-over papier-mâché heads continued to use these eyes until the pop-eyes and the pumpkin-heads of the 1880s.

Another type of the early papier-mâché formed the

Illustration 5. Wax-over papier-mâché head doll wearing original black and white lace dress. (Perhaps a half mourning outfit.) Germany. c.1850. 18in (46cm) tall.

head and torso, sometimes to the knees, of vertical front and back halves glued together. These are pictured in watercolors in a French toy catalog of 1810. A later descendant is the poupard, without arms or legs, with only the head painted and containing a few pebbles to make a rattle, sold in Paris about 1880 for one sou.

But the most popular form was a shoulder type of head, most often found on a stiff kid body with wooden forearms and lower legs. Due to their method of manufacture it was very easy to show the hair styles, so that a whole series of coiffures is found represented in them, including the fantastic ones of the 1825-1835 period. This has led to another myth, that these dolls were designed to send the latest hair styles to an expectant audience. They have been called "Milliner's Models" which carries the connotation that they are fashion models; again a misnomer. When found in original store clothes they are practically all dressed in a very cheap gauzy material known as tarlatan, current styles sketchily indicated and obviously intended for the mass toy market.

The English made their bid for the luxury class market with the hollow, heavy cast wax heads. Wax had been used for centuries for effigies, votive figures and portraiture. The cool English climate was favorable to wax which earlier had been used in thin coatings to give a nice complexion to wood or papier-mâché faces. Two immigrant families, the Pierottis and the Montanaris, brought the art of wax work from Italy, and at the 1851 Crystal Palace Exhibition the Montanaris won the grand prize with a group of most lifelike dolls. The inserted hair technique used on these dolls was not invented by the Montanaris but brought into popularity by them and immediately copied by other doll makers. The Pierotti family carried on the making of wax figures, such as window display mannequins, long after the wax doll had been superseded by other kinds. Baby dolls also came into prominence following the 1851 exhibition.

Back of all the romantic involvement which so many collectors have with the idea that the child's toy doll was a messenger of fashion, there is an undeniable fact — girls wanted their latest doll to resemble, be it slightly or elaborately, their mother's latest fashion in dress or coiffure. Furthermore, after the time of *Alice in Wonderland*, there were more baby or child-like dolls as well as ladies in miniature. This adherence to fashion was readily managed with dolls dressed at home and naturally was seized on by doll makers to promote seasonal sales. Dolls in the highest priced bracket are listed in the mail order catalogs of the 1880s as: "always dressed in the latest fashion" and "always dressed a la mode." Even peg-wooden dolls were carved with a high waistline in 1810 and a low corseted waist around 1835. With rare exceptions, dolls after 1800 were dressed, whether poorly or elaborately, with regard to the current style but they were toys and sold in toy shops, not as "milliner's models"

Illustration 6. Two wax-over papier-mâché head dolls. The doll on the left has wire pull eyes and original clothing. The doll on the right is attributed to Germany, c.1812. The doll on the left dates c.1845. Both dolls are 12in (31cm) tall.

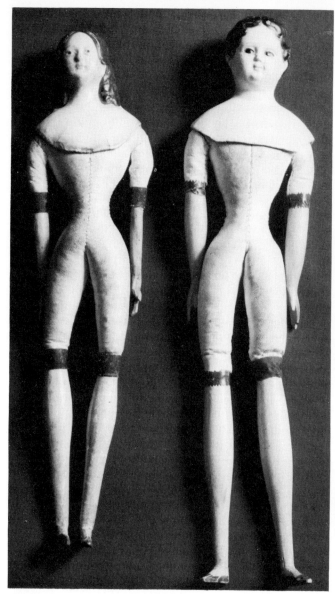

Illustration 7: Papier-mâché dolls with elaborate hair styles (Milliners models), kid bodies and wooden arms and legs. Germany. 19th century. 13in (33cm) to 14in (36cm) tall.

or "fashion dolls." When at all possible, original clothing should be preserved on old dolls and every effort made to distinguish between store clothes and home clothes. The former can be much finer and also much shoddier than the work of the home dressmaker.

In the late 19th century there were many experiments by doll makers trying to break into the market. There was a revival of wood, rawhide, leather, gutta percha, celluloid, metal, rubber and cloth. There were also talking, walking and singing dolls, and a variety of other mechanicals. Many of these experiments were made in America, but Germany was the most successful with its copy of the French bébé at a reasonable price for a child's toy. Millions were sold up until World War I.

Basically, the text of this book will be based on our personal collection, including all photographs, the importance of play in childhood, and in the social history of the times.

— *Ruth E. and Robert C. Mathes*

Illustration 8: Goodyear patented rubber doll with cloth body and kid arms. All original. America. c.1870.

18

Chapter 1

The Beginning

In the wonderful world of doll collecting, someone has to light the way. For us, that great lady was Imogene Anderson. It would be many years before we finally found her, but first we fell in love with her Letitia Penn doll.

We were married in 1916, and during those war years, Bob often traveled to Washington, D.C., on military projects for the Bell Telephone Laboratories. Ruth joined him on some of these trips, and spent time at the Smithsonian Institution. A chance meeting with a young curator named Malcolm Watkins, and the purchase of a postcard of *Letitia Penn*, plaything of a friend of the daughter of William Penn, and we were on our way. We assumed that the Penn doll was a part of the Smithsonian collection, so we made an appointment to view her. The museum staff assumed the same, but were embarrassed to report that the doll could not be found. In fact the Penn doll was never there, as we discovered many years later.

For a while our interest in toys revolved around the needs of our two children, Joyce born in 1920, and Robert Harris born in 1922. Ruth's studies at Columbia University under the influence of Dewey and others now had a practical application. Learning through doing was put into practice through the proper use of toys that had meaning for babies and young children. We made most of the toys when the children were very small. Rag dolls were important companions to sleep with, pull in carts, rock and cuddle. We found that the doll was the most important of all toys. (In our glossary, we want the term "doll" to mean a child's toy.)

We had built a home in the country where commuting by train to New York City was practical. When Joyce was five and Robert was three, we started the custom of occasionally meeting their father for lunch at Wanamaker's store in downtown New York City. First there was a train ride to Hoboken from Millburn, New Jersey. Then a subway ride under the Hudson River and a walk to the store.

After we had thoroughly explored Wanamaker, we began to visit other smaller shops in this downtown area. Joyce was always dashing ahead, and one day spotted a tiny shop that used doll heads to display wig styles. We went in and expressed our interest in the dolls. The owners were wig makers, newly arrived from Germany. They had brought a stock of early dolls with them in hopes of setting up a business in the city. They steered us

to the basement where we found boxes of wonderful old dolls of many varieties. In hindsight, this would have been a golden opportunity to start a fine collection. Joyce's choice was a fine china head with an elaborate hair style. (Later we gave this head a body, and used it to display costumes.) Robert's choice was a late Victorian dolls' house family, consisting of a mother, father, grandmother and a soldier. One lady had gray hair, one man had a mustache, and one man had on a hat that suggested part of a military uniform. To Bob, this was his family.

This dolls' house family started a project of building and furnishing and lighting a dolls' house that went on for years. As we look back, we realize that this was the motivation for our doll and toy collecting.

Pinocchio's Adventures, by C. Collodi, was our children's favorite book. The illustrations by Attilio Mussino were outstanding. They learned to read it slowly, after much repetition. We found that repetition had its place in child learning. And the book was worn out with use.

The next stage in our children's development also included dolls. Ruth had found a good celluloid boy doll head that seemed suitable, and with a proper body, dressed him to suggest a railroad conductor. Robert liked him and used him to ride on his electric train. It took two box cars to hold this doll, but it became an integral part of his railroad hobby.

Sewing was a family hobby, so when Ruth sewed clothing for Joyce, she in turn sewed for her *Patsy* doll. Old sheeting, colorful bias tapes, and scraps from her clothes were readily turned into doll clothing, all crafted by hand. An old hat box-type suitcase held *Patsy* and her growing wardrobe, making this a portable hobby. Most young girls are style conscious, and this was reflected in her homemade doll clothes.

High school and college absorbed both children, so interest in the doll collection became an adult avocation. We began to appreciate the toys of the Victorian period and their relation to folk art. Besides the bookshops in New York City that had captivated Bob since his arrival in that city in 1913, antique shops were now included in our browsing. Our sizeable book collection now had to make space for our growing doll collection.

Joyce entered William and Mary College in Williamsburg, Virginia, in 1938. When we visited her at college, we watched with interest the continuing restoration of

Illustration 9: A rare side view of the Letitia Penn wooden doll now in the collection of The Historical Society of Pennsylvania. *Photo from authors' collection.*

that historic town. It was there that we discovered the gallery showing Mrs. Abby Aldrich Rockefeller's folk art collection. Early portraits of children holding toys that we could identify, fascinated us. The folk art museum was yet to become a reality, one with which we were to become personally involved. On June 8, 1942, Joyce graduated from William and Mary. The next day she was married to Lieutenant Irvin L. Malcolm in the Christopher Wren chapel at the college. Another war had entered our lives.

In 1944, a new book, *The Album of American History*, by James Truslow Adams, had just been published. We bought it as a Christmas gift for Bob's mother. While thumbing through the pages, we were amazed to find on page 234 "The Penn Doll" in large letters. Below

the picture it said courtesy of Imogene Anderson of New York City. Here was the doll we had been seeking since World War I, and a clue to its whereabouts. To our delight, we found Imogene Anderson listed in the New York City telephone book. A call verified the fact that she was indeed the doll collector and owner of the doll that we had dreamed of seeing. When she heard our story, an invitation to tea followed, and a whole new world was opened up to us.

As Mrs. Anderson welcomed us into her New York City apartment, she smiled and said: "to my knowledge, Letitia Penn was never at the Smithsonian." We were directed down a hall to view Letitia. There she stood under a glass dome that had protected her all these years.

Her striking, fashionable dress with a skirt made of strips of different colored brocades, reminded us of an English wooden doll pictured in Carl Grober's *Children's Toys of Bygone Days*, illustration 51, "English Doll XVII Century." One of Letitia's arms was missing; otherwise she was in good condition. Letitia Penn has a permanent home now where she belongs, at the Historical Society of Pennsylvania, 1300 Locust Street, Philadelphia, Pennsylvania.

According to Janet P. Johl, the Penn Doll (circa 1730) was often called the oldest doll in America, and was originally in the collection of Mrs. Izole Dorgan of New York City. She and Mrs. Anderson had read about it in an old book on dolls. Mrs. Dorgan promised to pass the doll on to Mrs. Anderson if she ever parted with it, so that is how it became a part of her collection. Letitia Penn is 29in (74cm) high and wears a full court dress of the period, made of strips of brocade and velvet. The full skirt is stretched by crinoline. Perhaps this doll once belonged to Dr. Mahlon-Kirk of Maryland who lived on a grant of land given by Queen Anne.

As we passed down the long hall that led to the Anderson living room, glass cases filled with dolls made the hall one continuous gallery. Our quick glance caught sight of lady dolls that reflected period fashions, high hair styles and lovely clothing. This made us anxious to see more. Our questions revealed our ignorance, so at tea she told us of the bookstores she frequented in New York City. We came away with titles of books we should have, and names of stores where we could browse for further information. Now we were off and running as serious collectors.

Our friendship with Mrs. Anderson grew, and she would join us on some of our doll hunting expeditions. We found fertile ground in some of the antique shops of New Jersey and Pennsylvania. Our first Fortune Telling Doll came from one of these trips.

On this occasion we planned to drive deep into Pennsylvania with our guest and advisor Mrs. Anderson, who specialized in dolls with authentic historical associations. We owe much to her for orienting our activities in this hobby and on this trip we like to feel that she brought us good luck.

Starting from Millburn, New Jersey, our first stop was made in a roadside antique shop south of Flemington,

New Jersey. There we found a Jumeau doll in the original box with label. It was of the period just after the award of the gold medal to Jumeau and a label to this effect was printed on the stiff white kid body. We made a few more stops and found nothing else that day.

The next morning we really started hunting and it looked as though we were in for a disappointing day; a few trinkets, a couple of small china heads of slightly better than average glaze. By late afternoon we had worked back nearly to New Hope, Pennsylvania, where certain parts of Route 202 are almost lined with antique shops.

Here we were finally directed to a dealer at Lahaska, Pennsylvania, who had a rather modest shop, but had an interest in dolls and toys. Outside of some frozen Charlottes, there apparently was nothing on hand but parts which she was saving for a doll hospital. We bought three or four of the small frozen Charlottes and engaged in a conversation on doll collecting. Finally, as we were preparing to go, she remembered something upstairs that might be of interest to us. She brought down two dolls; one a wax coated papier-mâché "pop eye" and the other a 20in (51cm) jointed wooden doll.

Although soiled, crushed and disreputable looking, one arm missing from the elbow down, one leg gone from the knee down, she immediately impressed us as an aristocrat. Finely modeled head and shoulders, comb in hair, gray shadow spit curls marked her as belonging to the early peg wooden period when real craftsmanship went into the making of these dolls. Although badly cracked and peeling around her neck and back of the head, the heavy translucent enamel with the under tinted rosy cheeks was still in a fair state of preservation around the face. Later we found a photograph of this identical doll, same in face, form and jointing, reproduced in Max Von Boehm's *Dolls and Puppets* (Figure 120, page 129). That doll is (or was) in the Spielzeug Museum at Sonneberg, Germany. It had obviously come from the Grodner Tal. This is how we found our first Fortune Telling Doll. In Chapter 5 we will discuss Fortune Telling Dolls in greater detail.

In subsequent chapters, we will tell in more detail how we collected, where we collected and our need for research and knowledge in this remarkable world of dolls, toys and make-believe.

Illustration 10. Bisque Victorian dolls' house doll family. c.1890. Dolls range in size from 7½in (19cm) to 8in (20cm) tall.

Chapter 2

The Quest

OPPOSITE PAGE: Illustrations 11A and
11B: Peg-wooden doll with carved head
and ethnic Near Eastern clothing, found in
Venice, Italy, by the authors. (Front and
back views are shown.) Germany. 19th
century.

England

When we visited England in 1951, we seemed at first to have no luck in turning up anyone concerned with dolls. The antique shops we tried in London had none and disclaimed knowledge thereof, while at the big antiques show in London, one of the highlights of the Festival of Britain, there was not a vestige.

We had just been to Foyle's Bookshop (said to be the largest used bookshop in the world) on Charing Cross Road in London, where we had found a couple of copies of *Queen Victoria's Dolls*, one deluxe and one regular edition. Then we chanced upon a court off the main street made up of little shops, some showing antiques.

Attracted by a painting of a little girl with a toy in one window, we entered and were greeted by an elderly couple. The small room was so crammed with a bewildering array of things that there was hardly space to move about. We explained our interest, not only in dolls, but in books, illustrations, prints, and perhaps even a painting showing a doll. Upon closer inspection, the painting in the window, of mid-Victorian vintage, did not really intrigue us. Did they have any more?

Down from a storage rack near the ceiling came an unframed oil painting, 26 by 31in (66 by 79cm) in size. We had seen two or three oil paintings on the continent of a child with a doll, but none caught our interest to the point of purchase. This one did. We immediately felt that here was a typical semi-primitive unsigned painting done by one of those itinerant artists who provided many of the ancestral portraits of the late 18th and early 19th centuries.

This was definitely Empire peroid, both as to hair style and the white dress with blue ribbons for the sash and shoulder bows. The doll is naturally in similar costume with a red sash, coral necklace and bonnet. She wears golden shoes like her mistress.

Is the doll wooden, wax or papier-mâché? Unfortunately, artist's renderings of dolls' faces are more apt to be human rather than doll-like, so that we can get no clue there. If wooden, the straight stiff arm would indicate a late English wooden type instead of a Tyrolean (also known as Grödner Tal) peg-wooden, as the latter would most probably have had a bend at the elbow. A second possibility would be an early papier-mâché, one of those

with the stiff kid bodies. These, however, are rarely found with added hair, and the manner in which the lock of hair shows under the bonnet is not characteristic of this type. A third type of this period is the wax-over papier-mâché, the round-faced ones which look as though a late English wooden type had been used as a model from which the mold was made. While this type did usually have hair wigs, the waxing dimmed the effect of rouge on the cheeks. As the artist has portrayed this doll with bright red cheeks, we feel that it was most likely a late form of the indigenous English wooden doll.

These primitive paintings of England and early America can give us many hints on child life of their period. One of the largest collections of these paintings which we have had the opportunity to examine, is at the Abby Aldrich Rockefeller Folk Art Museum at Williamsburg, Virginia. In reviewing these with the curator, at that time Mrs. Mary Black, the idea was developed for a special Christmas showing — along with each such painting, an example of an antique doll or toy matching the one in the painting. Thus began a series of special doll and toy shows at Williamsburg each Christmas. In the Williamsburg paintings, a little girl was often shown with a little basket filled with flowers. Such a basket appears in the lower right hand corner of our painting. While we cannot rely on artists renderings of dolls and toys as to detail, we feel that much about the social history of the child may be learned from the paintings and prints in our art galleries. Thus, in the early 19th century, picking flowers was regarded as a suitable form of play or pastime for little girls.

But the little shop had more for us. This elderly couple kept in touch with a number of public museums and when these museums had a little surplus of some class of items, they managed to do some judicious trading. First to delight us was a Greek terra-cotta figure, a bit over 4in (10cm) long (see Illustration 2). Alas, the head was separate from the body and the arms were missing. The arms, however, had been pivoted and thus moveable, indicating that it was a toy or a child's God or spiritual figure. Its period is about first or second century B.C.

Next were a half dozen Coptic dolls, very crudely carved from bone. The Coptics were a Christian group in North Africa and these were said to date about 500 A.D. We selected two, one 3½in (9cm) long representing an adult, and the other a swaddling babe 2½in (3cm) long. (See Illustration 1.) We call them mother and child.

This couple had a second shop nearby, which had become so crowded that there was no space left to walk around, so they kept it locked. We went over and peered through the windows but could find nothing more.

Then in the outlying districts we finally got some nibbles. The effects of American demand were being felt. One midlands dealer asked us: "What's this craze that Americans are having over dolls?" (He had just passed on a fine wax doll, probably Montanari type, for five pounds.) Also at the Brighton show we later turned up some dolls that were not even being shown, but had been set aside for shipment to the United States.

At last, in Edinburgh, Scotland, we found a dealer who had heard of a dealer near Oxford, England, who was supposed to know about dolls, and if we had a chance to look him up when we got back, would we let him know. We would and we did. He was Mr. Roger Warner of Burford, England. A general antiques dealer, his stock of dolls was low but he did show us four pedlar dolls, not for sale, which he and his wife collected. From him we got some new viewpoints on these pedlars, on dolls in cases, and on the evolution of the English woodens. Finally he said: "If you can spare the time you should try to see Mrs. Early's collection. She lives nearby and recently got from me two wooden dolls of the time of Charles II. She is also working on a book on dolls." As our little motor trip in a rented car had no fixed itinerary we expressed great interest, and a phone call luckily secured an appointment for us shortly after lunch.

"Newland House" is on the edge of the village of Whitney. The stone house has its back to the road and the living rooms look out over a wide expanse of fields. We found Mrs. Early to be a charming, vivacious person. She greeted us cordially and, as we were ushered into the parlor, we saw that her dolls were fitted into the home, for there on chairs sat two very fine Montanari type waxes. Signs of the book in progress were soon evident, as a large table in the living room had many specimens spread out for study, and in her studio upstairs some were "sitting" for sketches to be made. For the next couple of hours we had the usual intense but disorganized discussion which results when hobbyists proceed from one item to the next.

Illustration 12: China *Alice in Wonderland* doll standing by limited editions of Lewis Carroll's books autographed by the original Alice. (From Mrs. Schenck's attic.) Germany, mid 19th century. 9½in (24cm) tall.

Illustration 13: Simon & Halbig bisque-headed doll with blonde wig and composition body, wearing dressmakers underwear. Early 20th century, the beginning of the character doll era. 22in (60cm) tall. (From Mrs. Schenck's attic.)

Her chapter on wooden dolls was of particular interest to us. It starts with a two-page transcript of a trial relating to some stolen dolls in 1733. Here is some new contemporary evidence on these early dolls. Two other contributions to the story of woodens are supplied by the photograph of a Courtier and Lady (Charles II period) and one of the figure of a priest of the Queen Anne period. The latter is shown clothed but we had the opportunity to examine the body closely during our visit. It is the most superb example of an artist's model that we have ever seen. The ball and socket joints are so perfectly finished that they move through all positions without loosening or sticking, something which we would have imagined to be possible only with metal. Here surely is one of the close relatives of the jointed Holy images and jointed dolls of continental origin.

We would not be true hobbyists if we agreed with all the ideas of any one author in this many-sided and still young field of collecting. We still disagree with Mrs. Early and many American authors who share the viewpoint that certain of the toy dolls after 1800 are to be thought of as "fashion dolls" rather than fashionably dressed toys. We will further discuss the evolution of the wooden doll in the research chapter of this book.

France

While the British Isles were celebrating their festivals, the French, in turn, developed a counter attraction — the two-thousandth anniversary of the founding of Paris. A striking feature of the Parisian affair was the organization of their window displays in the shopping areas. The several streets and boulevards were assigned definite historical periods as a unifying theme; one, the Middle Ages; a second, one of the Louis; another, the Revolution; still another, Napoleon III, and so on. With the simplest materials, they created the most intriguing displays. Naturally, where the theme indicated, they made use of dolls.

We were walking to the United States Embassy to see if the Bureau of Cultural Relations could secure us an entré to the Henri D'Allemagne collection, when one of these windows brought us to a halt. It was a small specialty shop for parasols and handbags. There, in the midst of a casually arranged group of precious furniture

and accessories, sat a period doll such as we had never seen before. A carved wooden head (we have an especial weakness for woodens) of an aristocratic grand-dame, stylish gown, and a large plumed hat made an eye catching ensemble. The lower part of the high hairdo, carved in the wood, showed horizontal hollow curls of the type popular in the reign of Louis XVI.

We went into the shop to request permission to photograph. They were most gracious, but, alas, the doll was only loaned to them, and they would have to ask the owner, Madame de Galéa, for approval. Could we call again in a few days after they had inquired? This was the first time we had heard Madame de Galéa's name and still it gave us no idea of her status as a collector. We said we would return after several days, little knowing that before we took that snapshot we would have seen her whole collection.

At the Bureau of Cultural Relations we met a most efficient young lady, but no one in the bureau had heard of the D'Allemagne collection. A little rapid fire telephoning in French brought no immediate results. All we could supply was the name of the publisher of the classic *Histoire des Jouets*. When we got back to our hotel that night we found an appointment all arranged! The extensive Henri D'Allemagne collection, only a small part of which is concerned with dolls, was housed in a large five-story building in downtown Paris. The famous collector had passed on shortly before our visit, but his son Jaques D'Allemagne took time from a busy day to guide us on such a visit as is described in his father's book, *The House of the Collector*.

A footman answered the door, and we were ushered into an interior so unkempt and forlorn that it was hard to believe that anyone lived there. We felt presumptuous as we were ushered upstairs where we were met by a young woman. She was Jacques wife and, unexpectedly, she was from California. She took us into their sunny apartment, which they had created in the midst of this tomb of a house.

With some embarrassment we offered to forgo our tour. But Jacques said: "No, we would be delighted — now that we know you!" He spoke very good English. We were shown room after room of exquisite things; ancient Persian rugs, delicate ironwork; and finally, the toys.

They were in a room depressingly dark, damp and

dirty. Jacques hastened to explain that this was in spite of all his efforts, that the house had been shut up during the war, and the task of rehabilitating this vast treasury was overwhelming and help impossible to find. We peered around us as best we could, for we had no flashlight, and saw many things that were familiar from the illustrations in D'Allemagne's books, but looking so lost and pathetic in the half dark. At the end of our tour, and noting our deep interest in the dolls, he said: "You must not leave Paris until you have seen Madame de Galéa's collection," and forthwith he made a telephone call to pave the way and gave us a card of introduction.

It developed that within a few days the collection was being shown to others and if we could come then, we would be welcome. We took a taxi from the hotel to 17 Ville de la Reunion, a country home, in order to be sure not to be late by getting lost in the underground. Two French antiques dealers had brought a few visitors, including another American couple, Mr. and Mrs. Grant J. Holt of Keene, New Hampshire. Neither Madame de Galéa nor her secretary could speak English and we spoke no French. Fortunately, one of the dealers spoke excellent English, was very familiar with the collection we were to see, and gave us good background information. He told us that she had also assembled an extensive group of Renoir paintings.

That Madame de Galéa was a collector in the grand manner was evident from the moment we entered the living room of her residence. That room in itself was a collector's item. Everything there — woodwork, furniture, rugs — was keyed down to emphasize the rare scenic wallpaper. One is tempted to call on Hollywood's adjectives to describe the effect, for it was at the same time gorgeous and exquisite. The wallpaper, hand blocked or painted in glowing colors, was all of the same pattern and yet had been miraculously searched out and transferred from the walls of a number of old chateaus. It portrayed garden party scenes of the Napoleon III period with the ladies and gentlemen shown on a large scale in elaborate costumes. It was only after the first impact of the room was absorbed that one became conscious of the collection of antique jewelry and small accessories in glass cases at several points about the room.

With Madame de Galéa's vivacious greeting of her guests, we were impressed with her vivid personality and her broad interest in human beings as well as things. She immediately made us feel at ease. Although her figure is short and mature, she gave an appearance of lightness and grace. Her white hair, worn high on her head, framed a face youthful in spirit. We especially felt her kindness. As we knew we had been added to the party at the last minute, we tended to stay a bit behind the group. But as Madame de Galéa noted this she was continually drawing us in for a better view of this or that.

Before going to see the dolls, we were shown the dining room for another example of specialized collecting. Here was a large sideboard laden with porcelain and majolica facsimiles of all types of food, both animal and vegetable. Everything from soup to nuts for a banquet of many courses was to be found there.

The dolls were housed in a small two-story cottage in the garden. We entered a foyer with cabinets displaying rank on rank of toy soldiers, as we recall it, about 100,000. The remaining wall space was papered with military posters and proclamations put out during past wars. In the rooms devoted to the dolls, the guiding spirit was display for beauty and dramatic effect, organization of the dolls into domestic and public scenes. Such use of the material tends to obscure some of the knowledge on historical development of interest to the doll student, but certainly it is most fascinating to the lay observer.

As we did not make notes at the time we cannot even approximate a complete description, but can only call to mind the more impressive features of each room. Among the dozen or so units in the first room there was, for example, a church wedding, complete with robed priest and attendants. The aristrocratic members of the family were finely dressed bisques, the poor relations, or perhaps servants, simply dressed papier-mâchés or woodens. The alter and other accessories were provided in painstaking detail. Similarly worked out was a small theatre on a scale of about one inch to the foot, about half that used for most of the others. There were about forty 6in (15cm) dolls in the orchestra and a group of actors on the stage. Additional groups were in boxes on a balcony. Again all types were used — bisques, chinas, woodens, and papier-maches, all carefully selected for uniformity in size.

A third striking scene was my lady in fine bisque at her toilette in an elaborately appointed boudoir. Her maids were papier-mâché. Still another was a tea party,

Illustration 14: Royal Berlin porcelain boy doll with dark brown painted hair, cloth body and kid arms and legs. Marked: "K.P.M." (Kongliche Porzellan Manufaktur.) Dressed in kilt. c.1840-1870. 15in (38cm) tall.

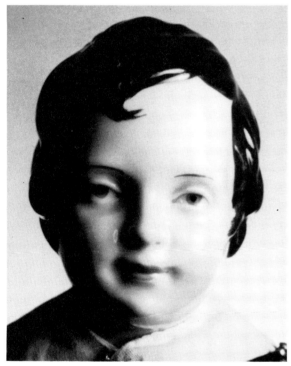

Illustration 15. Close-up of head of K.P.M. boy doll shown in Illustration 14.

which gave an opportunity for displaying finely dressed bisques and parians in a formal dining room setting.

On a much larger scale, and using the greater part of another room, was a dramatic simulation of a Parisian street scene with all its characteristic activities. Authentic backgrounds had been especially painted by an artist. This provided for the display of outdoor clothing of all types, as the characters ranged the whole scale from street *gamins* to persons of distinction.

All these scenes were, however, overshadowed by the imagination and care used in working out a creche or Nativity story. The only other creche which we had seen similarly created was at the Bayerische National Museum in Munich, Germany. While the museum had much more total material, it was divided between over a dozen separate scenes arranged for studying the national characteristics of creche (or Krippe) as developed in different parts of Europe. Madame de Galéa had lavished all her material upon a single large panorama. Painted backgrounds and three-dimensional models were combined to give a sense of depth. The illusion of distance and perspective was heightened within a relatively shallow space by using large figures in the foreground and progressively smaller ones to the rear, and scaling the accessory structures to correspond. Paths and roads led through scenes of all the activities of village and country life. The focal point was the stable with the Holy Child and the heavenly hosts above with the shepherds and their flocks in the background. As we recall it, most of the figures were of the types produced in southern Italy, whose artists were unsurpassed in delineating the emotions of awe and reverence which transfixed the individuals of all ranks intent upon this miraculous scene.

For especially rare and early dolls, of the type which we had first seen in the window display, there were separate period nooks with corresponding period furniture and accessories. In another room there were just dolls, arranged on stands as most collectors are apt to have them. Never, though, had we seen such a galaxy of fine parians, bisques and chinas as were here assembled. Among those single specimens were the larger dolls. Given a place of honor was a large figure ascribed to the XVI century and formerly in the Albert Goupil and Henri D'Allemagne collections. This is the figure shown on Plate XIII of Esther Singleton's book, *Dolls*, plate 32 of

Karl Grober, and Figure 101 of von Boehn's *Dolls and Puppets*. The latter book discusses this figure on pages 124 and 125 of the English edition.

While this assemblage of individual types indicated a preference for the more delicate and lovely types of dolls, there was a good sprinkling of other varieties. We noted particularly a number of early French papier-mâchés with glass eyes and teeth, the type on kid bodies with the exaggerated hips of the Napoleon III period. Also, there was quite a group of the solid wax head figures with beady black eyes which impress one as costume mannequins. These wore costumes ranging over a wide period, from Directoire to mid-Victorian, each so skillfully sculptured as to have an individual air of distinction.

Another section was devoted to dolls' clothes which displayed the fine French stitchery, not only in the outer costumes, but also in the large array of dainty underclothing. Separate heads, with a bit of lace or ribbon draped over the shoulders, were arranged in rows on shelves for showing the styles in millinery.

But our most vivid memory is of the room devoted to automata, several dozens of them, and of Madame de Galéa and her secretary dashing enthusiastically from one to another, winding them up. Then, to the medley of the many associated music boxes, the dancers jangled their tambourines, the jugglers juggled, the preacher delivered a sermon, the musicians sawed away at their violins, the acrobats tumbled, the magicians did their tricks, till one hardly knew which way to turn next.

By the end of our visit we felt a developing warm friendship, and when we said *au revoir* and goodbye the feminine half of this team of authors and Madame de Galéa did it in the characteristic French fashion of a hearty embrace and a kiss on both cheeks.

Today, the lions' share of this remarkable collection is housed in a new museum designed by Princess Grace in Monaco. It is now readily available to doll collectors from all over the world who are lucky enough to visit this charming city.

Italy

In Venice, as our gondola glided along the canals, we saw passing us a draper's shop, a very elegant establish-
Continued on page 41.

Patsy doll with wardrobe
and case. c.1930.

OPPOSITE PAGE: Two Parisiannes from France. *Left*, wearing tan dress, is 18in (46cm) tall. *Right*, wearing blue dress, and probably a Bru, is 16½in (42cm) tall. Original clothing, dating c.1860.

English oil painting of a child holding an English wooden doll with hair in the style of the Empire period. 30in (89cm) by 25in (63cm).

BELOW: Holy family found in Capri, Italy. *Joseph*, 9½in (24cm) tall. *Mary*, 8in (20cm) tall. *Babe*, 3in (8cm) tall. 18th century.

CLOCKWISE: Costumed wax figure of Sarah Bernhardt found in Scotland. Late 19th century. 14in (36cm) tall.

Costumed wax figure, seated, with mandolin. Probably from Paris, France. 13in (33cm) tall.

A restored plaster face English wooden doll with original clothing and body. Late 18th century.

German peg-wooden doll dressed and assembled in England as a pedlar with basket of handmade items. Such dolls were often made as wedding gifts. 10in (25cm) tall.

OPPOSITE PAGE: Three English wooden dolls, 12in (31cm), 12½in (32cm) and 14in (36cm) tall. The doll on the far left is all original with glass eyes. Mid 18th century. The doll on the far right is of the Empire period with painted eyes. The doll in the center is of a late period, dressed in much earlier period costume.

Three Schoenhut boy dolls, made in Philadelphia, Pennsylvania, from 1872 to 1925. *Left to right:* Home dressed doll, 16in (41cm) tall; 19in (48cm) tall doll is wearing his original kilt outfit; the undressed doll stands 14½in (37cm) tall.

Two puppets, one a "Punchinello" 22in (56cm) tall. The other stands 17in (43cm) tall. Both are made of wood and wear their original costumes. France.

Indian rod puppet (left), 22in (56cm) tall. Javanese rod puppet (right), 23in (58cm) tall.

Poured wax, wire pull doll with wax arms and legs and a cloth body. Original bodice. Homemade real hair wig. England. Early 19th century. 23½in (60cm) tall.

40

Continued from page 32.

ment with fine merchandise. At the back of the shop we glimpsed two dolls. Very excited, for we had so far found no toys in Venice, we begged the gondolier to go back.

The man in the shop spoke English. The dolls had been left with him to sell. They had been with him for a long time, and so far no one had much interest in them, including himself. He had no idea what they were, but we recognized them as late German peg woodens. He asked a very low figure, and we bought them with alacrity.

We were so interested in these dolls because they were unusual late examples, the high, carved hairstyles implied the pompadours of the 1870s, and the clothing is both unmistakably old and unmistakably Venetian. The flounced shirt is of fine ivory silk sewn over with intricate silver sequins, now black with age. The bodice is ivory damask, trimmed with brocaded ribbons, including three pendant pieces that form a stylized apron edged richly with blue silk, and encrusted with mother-of-pearl sequins and blue beads. She appears to be a peasant in festive attire, an impression strengthened by the formal headdress composed of gold braids, sequins and beads. It was clear that these dolls had been in Venice for at least 80 years, and provided us with yet another insight into the universal popularity of the wooden Grödner Tals during the 19th century, and the extent of their distribution. Only one of these dolls remains in our collection. She is 12in (31cm) high.

We had gone to Capri for three days rest from our journeyings, and Ruth asked if a hairdresser could come to the hotel to attend her. The accommodations were crude, but this could be accomplished. He spoke English very well, and while her hair was being washed, Ruth asked him if he knew of any old Religious figures or creche figures that we could see, and possibly purchase. His grandmother, he said, had owned an old family set, but the children had played with it and destroyed most of the figures. Grandmother, however, had rescued the three principal figures — The Virgin with the Holy Child and St. Joseph.

Later he left them at the hotel with a message that the grandmother would sell them for what seemed a small sum, if we were interested. We were indeed interested, for although the figures were no longer pristine they were family things, directly from the source.

The Virgin is an old figure, perhaps 18th century with the classic terra cotta head and inset glass eyes. The turn of the head and the swirling hair, besides the coloring, suggest the Neopolitan figures with which we are all familiar.

The other figures are different, perhaps made a little later. The naked baby is molded in terra cotta in one piece; the St. Joseph is slightly larger in scale, and his terra cotta head is most vigorously modelled. He and the babe have painted eyes. His paint is matte, like the French Santon figures, but there are traces of the original varnish under his collar.

Both adult figures have lost their hands and feet — at the mercy of the grandchildren presumably, and their exposed body structure, the usual hemp-wrapped wire, can clearly be seen.

The clothing is interesting because both adult figures wear coarse, late copies of the original tinsel trimmed garments. Under the Virgins coarse silk robe of blue and lilac is a much finer silk skirt trimmed with 18th century braid, all that is left, alas, of her original glory. It is encrusted with wax from the drippings of the votive candles.

St. Joseph's breeches are contemporary with the Virgin's robe, but his tunic of printed silks suggests 1910 or even 1920, made perhaps for the last time that these figures were taken seriously. The Virgin's outer mantle is of white silk with unhemmed fraying edges, perhaps put on by the children at an early stage of their play.

These figures encapsulate vividly a fragment of that Italian family's history: the treasures handed down, taken for granted and valued less and less; the indulged grandchildren using them, at first perhaps to reenact the Christmas story, with play which became rougher and more destructive until the grandmother's intervention. This whole little domestic drama, surely, has been repeated over and over during the last few generations.

From Mother Schenck's Attic

Our home was built in an historic section of New Jersey. Victorian houses were scattered throughout the wooded areas on our hillside. At the top of our acre we could see the New York City skyline in front, while wild deer from the adjoining state parkland roamed our back garden. We settled in our home when our son was a new baby, and Joyce was two years old.

Across the street from us were two rambling Victorian homes. Our afternoon outings became an adventure in meeting our neighbors. Mother Schenck, our elderly neighbor across the street, in Summer spent much time rocking on her front porch, and often invited us to join her. As long as we stayed on the veranda, the children could not harm her family treasures inside. We became close friends over the years, and gradually I became familiar with her lovely family antiques. Her father was a sea captain, and brought her treasures from all parts of the globe.

One day she asked me to go up to the attic for a box in a special place. She opened it and asked if we would like the little *Alice in Wonderland* period doll, c.1870. The previous owner was her aunt. I knew little about antique dolls at this point in time, but was delighted to accept her offer and expressed our appreciation. She had heard us discuss our family dolls' house project with it's late Victorian family. Years later we acquired two limited editions, *Alices Adventures in Wonderland* (1932) and *Through the Looking Glass* (1935), which were signed by the original Alice, Alice Hargreaves, in her old age. We have often displayed the doll and the books together as a delightful vignette.

As our friendship grew warmer over the years, this first trip to Mother Schenck's incredible attic became just one of many. Some of our loveliest dolls emerged from this attic.

The several Royal Berlin Dolls in the collection of Imogene Anderson charmed us with their beauty. For years we hoped to have at least one in our collection. In planning our trip to Europe, the one doll we longed to find in Germany was a Royal Berliner. Alas, this was not to be. Although we returned with about 75 other dolls,

and a series of antique trunks in which to ship them, this coveted treasure eluded us.

Back in New Jersey, we packed our belongings for our trip to California, and retirement. Before leaving we visited our neighbors, and said our final good-byes. At the home of Mrs. Stoneall, an elderly friend, we were presented with a box as we entered her house. To our amazement and utter delight the doll in the box, dressed as a Scots boy, was a Royal Berlin doll. We told her that this was the one treasure we had hoped to find in Germany, and were deeply touched by this gift.

Mrs. Stoneall was pleased to know that her special childhood treasure had found a good home. She was raised among the family heirlooms in her old family home in New Jersey. Her nanny allowed her to play with this doll only on Sunday. There was a special compartment in a trunk where he lived the rest of the week. After church, she was permitted to hold and rock this doll before changing from her Sunday best clothes. Mrs. Stoneall told us that the head had belonged to a Scottish artist who was an old friend of the family. He had added the body and clothes especially for her.

It must become obvious to everyone that dolls turn up in the most unexpected places. There are an abundance of stories, too numerous to mention, on how we discovered some of our favorite treasures. Dealers are the most obvious source, but one doll was acquired from a friend of our dentist. Others have been barterd and swapped for goods or services. Until we sold two patent heads to the Margaret Strong Museum in Rochester, New York, we have never sold any part of our collection. Some we have given away, but we never felt our collection was a commercial venture. The joy has been in the collecting and the research. Our friends are all familiar with our hobby, and have assisted us in many of our finds.

Chapter 3

Understanding:
The Ultimate Rewards of Research

Research Applied to Dolls

The general process of expanding knowledge is commonly referred to as "research." This word has been much bandied about in recent years, what with Congress appropriating billions of dollars for that activity in many fields of defense, health, education, and agriculture. To many persons the word is most familiar as applied to something called "market research" or poll taking by politicians. In these forms it simply means the rounding up of opinions. In scientific and technological circles, however, the objective of research is not opinion or belief, but knowledge.

In some sixty years of collecting, first dolls and later toys, we have tried to keep in mind this objective of knowledge. We have been inspired by a definition of research given by H. D. Arnold, one of the first research directors of the Bell Telephone System. In the Lowell Lecture in Boston, Massachusetts, on January 5, 1932, he said: "Research is not constructing and manipulating; it is not merely investigating or experimenting; it is not getting the facts; although each of these activities may have an indispensible part to play in it. Research is the effort of the mind to comprehend relationships which no one has previously known. And in its finest exemplifications it is practical as well as theoretical, trending always toward worthwhile relationships, demanding common sense as well as uncommon ability....These are the three requirements of research: the spirit of adventure, the wit to question, and the wisdom to accept and use."

While the details of this statement were shaped by the physical sciences, its spirit is being increasingly applied to the humanities and social sciences of which our hobby may be regarded as a part. We may draw heavily upon them for our initial data and may hope to bring new knowledge to the general store.

The philosophical approach to the scientific methods of research was stated by Sir Francis Bacon thus: "If we begin with certainties we shall end in doubts; but if we begin with doubts we shall end in certainties." The method to be applied is indicated by the title of a book by a modern scientific philosopher, Karl R. Popper, *Conjectures and Refutation*. In brief, from initially available data, one forms a theory or hypothesis or conjecture. If this theory is productive it will raise questions whose answers will either support or refute it. The latter is especially important for only when a conjecture stands up against a refutation may it be regarded as valid.

Before taking up specific illustrations of the application of the method, we will note, with some general commentary, six of our most available sources of data upon which we may draw to establish a conjecture.

1. The doll itself.
2. Source material, such as letters, diaries, account books, genealogies, city directories, catalogs, advertisements, periodicals, patents and copyrights issued, paintings, museum collections, and so on.
3. Published literature in the humanities, especially on child life, fashions, manners, customs, folk art, and so on.
4. Discussions with specialized experts from museum curators to antiques dealers in many diverse areas such as fashions, fabrics, laces, buttons, finishes, arts and crafts, porcelain, religious figures, toys in general, puppets, and so on.
5. Previously published books and articles on dolls.
6. Family stories coming with the doll.

The usefulness and reliability of these sources is subject to great variation with source No. 1 perhaps the most valuable and No. 6, though helpful, often quite misleading, requiring independent verification. For example, the late Mrs. William Walker of Louisville, Kentucky, once told us that after hearing a family tale she always went to the graveyard to check the dates on the tombstones. In a small museum in New England we noted an incorrect labeling probably due to a family legend. Four small 1¼in (3cm) peg-woodens were marked as having been made by a dentist. Close scrutiny revealed that one was a very fine Tyrolean peg-wooden of about 1825, while the other three were credible but still rather crude copies. An elderly woman sent us a well-worn wooden doll with the story that her great, great grandfather had carved it in 1830. The date was correct but despite its dilapidation we had no trouble in seeing that it was a Tyrolean peg-wooden of that time and not a primitive.

When such unverified family stories become imbedded in the pioneer books on doll collecting (source No. 5) they can become troublesome. Thus, on page 93 of *Dolls of Three Centuries*, St. George wrote: "In the author's collection is an English-made wooden doll, dating about 1786. The body is painted red." She also stated it was very rare as she had heard of only one other. Probably a family story was responsible for her being so specific as to both origin and date. Comparing her photograph with plate 33 of Hercik's book, *Folk Toys*, we find these red-bodied dolls with leather or cloth joints were made in western Bohemia and, judging by the hair style, not earlier than the second quarter of the 19th century. They continued to be made in much the same style until around World War I. Shortly after St. George's book was published, a friend wrote us: "A Florida dealer had just offered me a red-bodied wooden doll for $150.00. Am I crazy, or is he?" Such stories thus could be very expensive. We suspect that, unfortunately, there are many such stories still unchallenged. So beware; question and verify.

More broadly, as regards source No. 5, our judgment is that the reliability of published doll literature varies from excellent to poor. In general, books written after years of experience in the museum or antique field are of the greatest value. Those written out of a short time collecting enthusiasm will often have assembled much useful material, but also contain many hasty and incorrect conclusions. Even among the more experienced writers a tale may be passed along without due regard for the original context, from Fournier to Claretie to D'Allemagne to Singleton to St. George and so on to the quickie magazine articles. A common failing is quoting without question the opinion of a collector and making judgments from photographs only.

Among the pitfalls to look out for in existing publications is the distortion caused by an incorrect translation from a foreign language. Thus von Boehn supplies us with many useful relationships due to his solid background in social history and styles. On page 150 of the first English edition of his *Dolls and Puppets* it is correctly stated that the French revolutionary and the Napoleonic wars interfered with the sending of fashion dolls, and that the need for such dolls had been dissipated by the introduction of the colored fashion plate. It then goes on, "Their use, however, has not wholly ceased." The use of the present tense implies that they were still being used at the time von Boehn was writing, in the 1920s.

What von Boehn actually wrote was, "Ganz aufgehort hat der Gebrauch darum doch nicht." The correct transla-

Illustration 16: **Red body wooden dolls with leather joints made in Bohemia. 19th century. 6½in (17cm), 13in (33cm) and 9½in (24cm) tall.**

tion of the past tense is, "Yet their use had not for this reason completely ceased." This use of "has" instead of "had" may be one of the reasons why we are now encumbered with the awkward term "so-called French Fashion Doll."

Another source of possible misinterpretation occurs in publications which use artists renderings instead of photographs. The artist often dramatizes or prettifies the original. Those whose expectations are raised by the charming watercolors in Miss Lowe's book *Queen Victoria's Dolls*, may be disappointed in seeing the drab but quaint originals on exhibit in London, England. When on compares the brilliant watercolors reproduced in D'Allemagne's *Histoire des Jouets* with photographs of the same items in his *La Maison D'un Vieux Collectioneur*, one could hardly identify them as the same if it were not for the captions. The same difficulty will confront the researcher who studies the watercolors of dolls and toys collected in the Index of American Design in the National Gallery in Washington, D.C.

We have recently had an upsurge of activity in source No. 5, books and articles on dolls which have digested for our convenience much of the material in sources 2 and 3. It has taken a great deal of effort and perseverance to produce these and we are grateful to have them available. It is inherent in the nature of the research process, however, that we must question some of the conclusions

Illustration 17: Two German peg-woodens of the finest period, early 19th century. The oldest, 7in (18cm) tall, has windblown bob. The 9½in (24cm) tall doll has a comb in her hair. Both are all original.

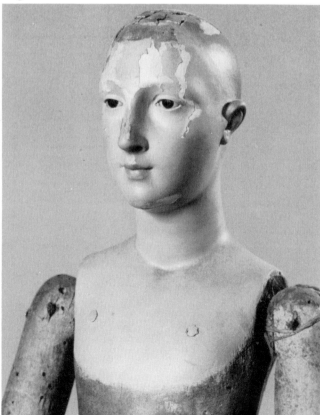

Illustrations 18A and 18B: Madonna of the Rosary (two views), holding a single bead in her right hand; moveable arms with hook fasteners. Probably Spanish. 18th century. 33in (84cm) tall.

46

stated. We hope that the possibility or probability of being so questioned will not deter further publications. We recall talking with C. Malcolm Watkins of the Smithsonian Institution about our hesitancy in publishing. He encouraged us to get out on a limb, to stimulate discussion. Edward P. Alexander, a vice-president of Colonial Williamsburg, also pointed out that the dedicated amateur has provided the initial impetus to many phases of museum collections, even though much of this early work had to be corrected later. And sometimes the amateur scores over the professional.

Now to get back to the most important category, the doll itself. As the late Mrs. R. C. Williams, better known to many of us by her pen name "Darcy," often said: "I always let the doll tell me about herself first." This presupposes a fair knowledge of the social history, the styles, materials, and craftsmanship of different periods and cultures (sources 3 and 4). This is the only common language of the doll, and to translate it we must become familiar with the background of her place and time. For the European scene the four volumes of von Boehn's *Modes and Manners* provides a good beginning.

Of all the classes of dolls, the woodens have most intrigued us. This special interest began when we traced down Letitia Penn to Mrs. Imogene Anderson and enjoyed her generous counsel while studying her remarkable collection. Later we had the advantage of discussions with "Darcy" and Mrs. Helen Hinkley of Redlands, California, who collected only woodens.

There has been much confusion, disagreement and error in the literature on wooden dolls. While much is still obscure, we feel that out of our study there had emerged a pattern which runs contrary to preconceived ideas which had caused much of the mixup. Strangely, yet logically, it has been followed by two distinct lineages of the woodens. This pattern is that, within the period from which specimens are available for collecting, there has not been an evolution from crudity to refinement but rather the reverse. We call this, "The Decline and Fall of the Wooden Doll." On an extended trip in the Winter of 1959-60 we presented this thesis as a slide-talk to many doll clubs and museum personnel. A part of this text is based on that talk modified by new material and ideas developed in discussions along the way.

Of our two lineages, the first is commonly called the

Illustration 19: Peg-wooden doll. Germany. 19th century, 17in (43cm) tall.

Queen Anne, or the blockhead type, and the second, among others, the penny wooden or the Dutch doll. As there are certain dangers in these usages we suggest, for the first "English Woodens." It covers the whole period in which they were made. Unless a doll is extraordinarily documented, as practically none are, one cannot place it in Queen Anne's reign which was for only twelve years. This English family of dolls appeared in the 17th century and disappeared early in the 19th with gradual changes in the style in which it was executed.

For the second major type of term "Peg-Wooden" will be used. These developed on the Continent in the late 18th century, were imported into England in huge numbers during the 19th century, and were made for some time into the 20th century.

The earlier reference to babes in pedlar's packs and to babes of clouts (or rags) indicates that there were toy dolls of simple and humble types in England in the 17th century, and very likely earlier. For example, a 17th century turned figure of the time of James I is shown on page 109 of Alice K. Early's book, *English Dolls, Effigies and Puppets*. She quotes on page 90 from a court trial in 1733 on stolen dolls: "14 naked babies and 2 dozen dressed babies and one jointed baby." The specific mention of "one jointed baby" implies that the others were simply turned figures, as the maker was a turner by trade who also made furniture. So, perhaps even well into

Illustration 20: **Costumed wax figure made in Paris, France. 19th century. 14in (36cm) tall.**

the 18th century jointed dolls may have been in the luxury class.

In the wooded areas of central Europe similiar crude toys were being whittled or turned in the homes of the peasants. Higher quality forms would be the product of guilds into which the arts and crafts were then tightly organized. Thus, woodcarving was the product of one group, painting of another, and costuming by others. There was not the present high degree of nationalism, many languages being found in one kingdom, and overall was the unifying influence of the Church. Hence, apprentices, at the end of their indentures, might spend their "Wanderjahre" in distant countries and perhaps settle down with their craft knowledge far from home. Thus it is not surprising that in the pages of Karl Grober's *Children's Toys of Bygone Days* or the *Studio* special issue (Winter 1932) "Children's Toys of Yesterday," we note dolls in the museums of many countries which have a

general resemblance. Unless a specific doll of these early centuries has a history we would in many cases be uncertain of its point of origin.

Furthermore, as is quite natural, few dolls of the humbler sort have been preserved due to their crudity and small value. So most of our knowledge and the relatively few specimens in collections from the 1600s are of the more aristocratic types. We also know that by the end of the century wood sculpture and finishing had developed to a high degree of perfection. This appears in the work of the more expert craftsmen making religious images and artist's mannequins. For the former, fine finishes of varnish enamel over gesso were developed and, for the latter, the ingenious ball and socket jointing enabling the figure to assume almost any pose. As most religious figures were to be dressed, often only the face, hands and feet were finished. Bodies were generally crude with few or no joints. Artist's models, on the other hand, were left unfinished but considerable care was given to the proper body proportions, both male and female. In the making of dolls we can trace the influence of both religious and lay figures.

An interesting example of the doll's direct communication is the case of a doll pictured in *Doll News* of May 1961, and identified in the captions as 18th century Russian. The identification was made solely on the basis of a potter's mark of three lines and a dot. The style of the head and body and general construction led us to feel this doll was made in the 1840s. Furthermore, the description of the doll said that it had deep pink flesh tones while the same handbook in which the potter's mark was found stated that the St. Petersburg glaze had a bluish character. This led to a questioning of the first conjecture. Extensive correspondence finally developed that the three lines were a hasty slurred form of the three wavy lines used as a mark by Royal Copenhagen, with which they had used the added dot only in the years 1840-45. With the correct information they were still very fine and very rare dolls.

Perhaps the best way to learn a doll's language is to visit as many collections as possible, private and museum. Relatively few museum curators are as yet familiar with dolls, but they can give us invaluable information as to materials, finishes and styles of different periods. Sometimes the doll's language is an odd dialect and will be understood only by persons of a particular background.

Illustration 22A: Church figures of Tobias and the Angel. Red clothing very old cotton brocade, lined with manuscript paper. (Probably not original clothing.) These are ancestors of the doll. Tobias is 10in (25cm) tall; the Angel is 21in (53cm) tall. 18th century.

Illustration 22B: Tobias and the Angel unclothed. All wood bodies. Germany.

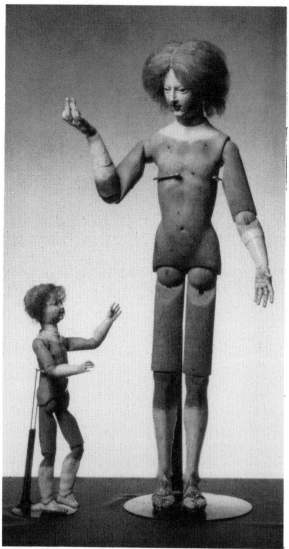

Thus Sister Magdalen Mary of the Art Department of Immaculate Heart College, commented on one entry at the UFDC Convention in Los Angeles: "What is an angel doing sitting in a chair?" This figure's information was in the disposition of its wind-blown hair, corresponding to a horizontal flying position. She looked very uncomfortable dressed as a court lady. This error in classification was not noticed by the judges.

With this brief consideration of some of the strong and weak points of our principal source of data, we would now like to outline a more detailed application of the questioning and refutation process to several pertinant examples.

The first of these is the "Dutch Doll," also known colloquially as Flanders babies, penny wooden, peg-wooden, German pipestem, wooden Betty, stick doll, and so on. The two major usages, carrying an ascription of origin, were inherited from the early days of poor communication when English traders bought them at the great fairs, such as Nuremberg, Germany (Deutch=Dutch) and Bruges, Belgium (Flanders). Once a term got estab-

lished in England it hung on. It was further entrenched in early doll literature by the couplet:

"What the children of Holland delight in making,
The children of England delight in breaking."

Here we will abstract briefly some of the highlights of the process of refutation of these early conjectures. The challenge began with Miss Jennie Abbott, Historian of the Doll Collectors of America, in an article she prepared for the club's manual, *Dolls,* for 1946. Miss Abbott apparently possessed a goodly portion of what Bertrand

Russell called "The Will To Doubt" as contrasted with "The Will To Believe."

Miss Abbott granted the possibility that these dolls might have been made in any of the four major German wooden toy making centers — Sonneberg, Berchtesgaden, Oberammergau and the Grödner Tal, but the only specific information which she found placed them in the last. As each of the four areas had distinctive styles of work we may then reasonably place them in the last. The fact that they turn up in so many places may be explained by the fact that they were wholesaled through Nuremberg (from which came their French name, Nuremberg fille).

A second worker who made important contributions to upsetting the original conjecture that these dolls came from the Lowlands was Mrs. R. C. Williams. Her insistence on factual data led her to take samples of the wood from these dolls to wood experts who, by microscopic evaluation, determined that they were made from a small type of pine commonly called the Siberian Pine, which grows on the slopes of the Alps and is not found in the Lowlands.

But the most conclusive evidence was turned up by Raymond J. Walker, who published in the December 1956 *Hobbies* a digest with lengthy quotes entitled "A Tribe Of Toymakers." Reference to the original article shows it to be a most readable account of a visit to the Grödner Tal. It was published in England in *Leisure Hour* in 1875, and reprinted in this country in the March 4, 1876, issue of *Littel's Living Age.**

At that time Miss Margaret Howitt searched into the history of woodcarving in this isolated valley and her findings reinforce, and somewhat overlap, the later research by Miss Abbott and Mrs. Williams. The Grödners, she found, were a race apart, being neither German, as the Austrians of whose empire they were then a part, nor Italian where, with their valley's name changed to Val Gardena, they were a rebellious minority group. They spoke a Romanesque language related to some of the dialects in Switzerland. They began about 1703 with the carving of picture frames from the Siberian Pine, plentiful on their mountain slopes. The work extended to crucifixes and household articles, and finally to toys and dolls. The valley was so isolated that in the early days all goods were packed out by pedlars.

As they prospered, these pedlars set up merchant houses in many of the principal cities — first to the south in Italy, Spain, and Portugal, and then to the north in the Low Countries and Germany. One even reached Mexico City before the end of the 18th century, and a couple got as far as New York City and Philadelphia, Pennsylvania, to set up toy shops there. Oddly enough, none of these strange people, holding strongly to their own language, settled in England, but a member of a Grödner firm established in Nuremberg, Germany, visited London regularly. All this fits in with what was mentioned earlier about the dolls receiving the name "Dutch" from the location of the wholesale distributor.

In the 1870s, the production of these dolls was still an extensive business, with shipments to England, the largest customer for them, running as high as "60 to 70 hundred-weight the week." Local agents in St. Ulrich (now in Northern Italy and renamed Ortise) coordinated the piece-work with which these dolls were made, often in a part-time operation along with farming or other employment. Miss Howitt describes the painting of faces by a girl while tending a fruit stand. She might do a hundred dozen a week for which she received a farthing a dozen. Out of this she had to supply her own colors and size. This last confirms what Grober relates about the painting of early toys. They were done in watercolors then dipped in varnish. Mrs. Williams experimentally reproduced this process whereby the remarkable translucent finish was obtained in the early 19th century. Some rare few of these have come down to the present with scarcely a crack or a blemish.

The history of importing peg-woodens from the Tyrol did not end with Miss Howitt's time. In January 1961, the Lanchester Marionettes, 39 Henley Street, Stratford-on-Avon, Warwickshire, England, issued a two page brochure, *Collected Information about Dutch Dolls.* They quote a letter from a Mr. Randall who imported them for years: "The merchants were always German firms trading in these areas and the firm from whom I buy them has been trading in them for 150 years. They were of original German stock and used to market them through their German branch at Nuremberg prior to 1914. Since then they have been sold from their Italian

---

*Margaret Howitt wrote an article entitled "Tribe of Toymakers," which was published in the 1875 issue of *Leisure Hour*, describing the making of wooden dolls in the Tyrol.

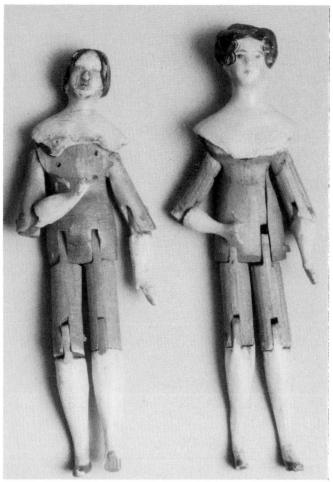

Illustration 23: **Peg-wooden dolls with "alien" heads. 7in (18cm) tall.**

branch in the Tyrol. As regards construction, the smaller ones had simple joints, as the sizes got larger more elaborate jointing was used and in the larger sizes, 22 to 24 inches, the wrists were all jointed with ball and sockets, secured by pegs, and the features were better carved, such as ears and eye-sockets." This Randall letter definitely makes the source of these dolls the Grödner Tal since about 1800, as it was this part of the Tyrol given to Italy at the end of World War I.

There remained one other major problem with regards to these dolls which was a cause for perplexity, their chronology. The clue to the key relationship which we feel has unravelled most of this problem was given to us by an antiques dealer, Roger Warner of Burford, England, with respect to another family of wooden dolls in England — the English Woodens. Changing social, economic, technological and competitive conditions will often modify what was once a finely-crafted item for the luxury trade into a much cruder form for the mass market. The 7in (18cm) peg-wooden in Illustration 17, Right, of the Directoire Period (1800's), shows what nicely carved features even such small dolls had at the time of their introduction. They were finished with a fine translucent varnish. Larger sizes were fitted with ball and socket joints (suggesting that their prototype was the artist's model). They had even more elaborately carved faces. By the middle of the 19th century (about the height of their

popularity for the mass market) wooden dolls had become so hastily made that we now think it best to use the term "Tyrolean Peg-Wooden" as there were other kinds of dolls and figures which used pegs for joining. The preconception that dolls should evolve from crudity to perfection, has caused much confusion. We have seen them labeled in museums as a Kentucky stick doll or a Cape Cod doll, and one even turned up as Mexican folk art. When the author of a new book accepts the data on museum labels, or the statements of private collectors, many of this type of doll are still being incorrectly classed.

In one instance is shown an early (17th or 18th century) Holy Child. This figure had originally been completely carved in most naturalistic detail and enamelled all over. We had this image with us on our trip and were shown for comparison two others of the same size and with practically identical features. Almost the only difference was that one had no joints and the other had arm joints only at the shoulder. Both had been crudely emasculated by broad chisel gouges. One had the waist somewhat narrowed but equally crudely. Both were said to be Spanish or Portugese and legend had it that such images had been mutilated as the result of a religious conflict.

The feminization of the image was, however, done by whittling with finesse so that a stylish 18th century gown could be fitted to it. It might well have been adapted to use as a fashion doll. This figure may also have been an example of early use of the inserted hair technique, as we found embedded by their ends several hairs in the remnants of hard wax on the head. When it came to us, the sandalled feet were encased in suede shoes. It had been supplied with an elaborate wig with braids coiled flat to the head, and a calico gown and bonnet of the 19th century. It was now a child's toy and the Munich (Germany) antiques firm first reported it to us with the self-contradictory statement: "A wooden doll of the Biedermeier period with the fine enamels of the 17th and 18th centuries." It is not unlikely that under various conditions many original sacred images have been converted to secular use.

In Illustration 18 is shown another church image (probably Spanish) which displays the classic perfection of early carving. By the bodice line it appears to be 18th century. One might suspect it to have been made for a lay figure such as a fashion doll, if it were not for one bead of the rosary carved integral in her right hand and the piercing of the left hand to hold the emblem which distinguished that particular personage. Only the hands and head have the fine enamel, but the rest of the figure is painted. This painting of the body we have observed to be characteristic of sacred images of Spanish or Mexican origin. In the more northern parts of Europe the bodies were generally left in the natural wood.

It is interesting to note that this refinement in carving was carried over into doll making to a greater degree in Continental Europe than in England. Henry VIII had begun the separation of the Catholic Church from control over the state, and the rapid trend to Protestantism removed a principal reason for skilled image carvers. Indeed, under Cromwell, images became anathema. The Continental trends will be considered later in relation to the origins of the peg-wooden doll, and we will take up first the English wooden doll of the 18th century, plus or minus a few decades.

It was in connection with the English wooden dolls that we first got the idea of the negative evolutions among woodens. We saw, at the Victoria and Albert Museum, some marked "1st half of the 18th century" (Figs. 2 and 3 of the V. and A. pamphlet, *Small Picture Book #16*) and also a group of three (Fig. 6 Ibid. The School of Scandal Dolls) marked last half of the 18th century. But we were puzzled because the former were of so much finer craftsmanship than the latter. Why?

The answer was supplied (in 1951) by the aforementioned, knowledgable Roger Warner at Burford, Oxfordshire, England. The Industrial Revolution, he pointed out, was getting well underway by 1750 with the accompanying growth of a large middle class who could afford to buy moderate-priced toys for their children. Before that time, good dolls were a luxury item and the carver spent considerable time on expressive features for the head, and the enameller would apply many coats of finish over a base of gesso. With a mass market came mass production methods; heads became more spherical and were left almost as they came from the lathe with very little carving. The faces were still given an excellent enamel over gesso finish almost to the end of the period. While the bodies from the beginning had been mostly crude, as the dolls were to be dressed, the later bodies became still

Illustration 24: Primitive Dutch doll all handcarved in Holland, including the wooden shoes. Cloth body. Original clothes. 19in (48cm) tall.

cruder and flimsier.

With this criterion (and such hints as come from family histories) we have, from examining illustrations in the literature and specimens in museums and private collections, arrived at a pattern of development which appears reasonable to us. Several types or stages will be described in order of time. We suspect considerable overlapping may occur as each innovation would not cause an immediate termination of an older form. This would be particularly true in an industry in the hands of individual craftsmen.

Stage 1:
The Carved and Painted Eye Type

Some of the earliest of these dolls had quite realistic features, with eyes carved into the wood and painted. The classic example of this stage is Fig. 1 in the Victoria and Albert Museum pamphlet (also well reproduced in Mrs. Early's book, Fig. 37, and on page 87, No. 5 in *Dolls of Three Centuries* by St. George). It is dated about 1690 and is said to have been given to Queen Anne herself. The captions and photographs do not bring out that the eyes are painted.

In this country among the three fine English Woodens from the Elizabeth Day McCormick Collection in the Museum of Fine Arts in Boston, Massachusetts, there is an exceptional example. The eyes are so finely painted with their highlights that from a photograph one would think they were glass eyes. This figure has joints at the knees. The other two dolls have glass eyes. One has been reproduced in Fig. 2104 on page 749 of *The Book of Costume* by Millia Davenport. In the group of 18th century wooden dolls at Colonial Williamsburg there is one of the early sculptured and painted eye type. We have seen two of these "Stage 1" dolls in private collections; one in that of Mrs. Singsen in New England, and the other in the collection of the late Marie Matheson, now on display in Bea De Armond's Hobby City Doll Museum on Route 39, a few miles south of Buena Park, California. Both of these dolls have a family history dating them before 1700. One of the female dolls in the Boston group has well-turned calves, but for the most part they have relatively crude legs. Until about the close of the 18th century, these were set into squarish hips with mortise and tenon joints.

In both Stage 1 and Stage 2 types, with the eye sockets well recessed, the eyebrows are painted in with a sweeping curve following the carving. In the Victoria and Albert Museum doll there are no auxiliary lines or dots to indicate hair, but one male doll has fine lines of a lighter tint drawn over the main arch and pointing slightly away from center.

Stage 2:
Eyebrows and Eyelashes

In the Stage 2 dolls these lines and dots are beginning to be more formalized. The head of one doll in Colonial Williamsburg not only shows the large black pupil-plus-iris eyes of Stage 2, but also the beginnings of the conventionalized treatment of the eyebrows and the eyelashes. The eyebrow appears much as an abstract drawing of a millipede and rows of closely placed dots just above and below the eyes indicate the lashes. This conventional treatment emphasizes the too close appearance of the eyes; some even refer to these dolls as cross-eyed. The well shaped lips, ears and chin are typical of the carving found on the first two types, though facial characteristics vary considerably between examples.

On display in the American Wing of the Metropolitan Museum of Art, New York City, is one of the most beautifully preserved of these early 18th century dolls. The oval face with the overly high forehead (a style achieved by plucking the hair) marks the end of a certain kind of beauty dating back to the 16th century. At the same time the "fork hands" introduce a kind of hand often provided for these dolls through the mid-18th century. Just below and to the right of her watch is a large "bullseye," the handblown pane of glass in the cabinet door. This door has possibly never been open since she was installed. Another doll of this class, which has remained in its own specially fitted dome for its whole history, was in the collection of the late Mrs. R. C. (Marjorie) Siebert of Rochester, New York, and now in the collection of Peggy Lancaster.

Stage 3:
The Mass Produced or Georgian Doll

von Boehn, in his *Dolls and Puppets* was quite correct in the single comment he made on these dolls: "English dolls have disproportionately large heads." He should also have added: "disproportionately small hips" (color photo on page 39 and Illustration 25). This became especially true with the rising demand for larger numbers at smaller costs toward the middle of the 18th century. The minimum of time and effort resulted when head, shoulders and hips were all turned to nearly the same diameter. It is possible that the flat back was automatically produced by simply mounting a rectangular block off-center on the lathe. While there is some variation in the shapes of the necks and bosoms, in general the heads become spherical and the amount of carving time less as time passes by.

The treatment of the eyes becomes still more conventionalized, a fine curved line with a parallel row of dots for the eyebrow and tiny rows of dots in an almond shape for the lashes. The apparently universally used glass eyes become smaller and more protuberant and still have a single black center, but now with relatively more white showing on each side. This has been called the simple eye to distinguish it from the more complicated form with a colored iris. This simple eye continued in use for many years with the wax-over papier-mâché doll heads down to the pop-eyed dolls of the 1880s. Most of the dolls found in collections and labeled "Queen Anne" belong to Stage 3.

In addition to being made for toys, these dolls were also used as "bagman's dolls" or mannequins to display the latest dress fabrics. This was perhaps the genesis of some of the cruder, heavier types often referred to as bedpost dolls, from the resemblance of the head to the finial of a bedpost. On the head of one of these figures in the Abby Aldrich Rockefeller Folk Art Collection at Williamsburg, Virginia, the features are pulled abnormally close together and the glass eyes have blue irises.

It may never be possible to determine the period of a particular specimen on the basis of crudity alone, for the simple reason that several qualities were probably being made at any one time for the luxury and the lower class markets. The same situation may be noted on the Continent where a higher quality of craft in making dolls is most generally to be noted.

Stage 4:
Molded Faces and Pointed Torsos

These are the last of the line. Apparently they represent an attempt to make a doll as cheaply as possible to stave off competition from the peg woodens now being imported from the Continent. They are a relatively small doll, the heads being 1 to 1½in (3 to 4cm) in diameter. Instead of having the hips cut off squarely to provide a place to mortise in the legs, the lower body is tapered in triangular section to a point. The legs are hung on each side with a transverse wire or string, and are usually little more than splints with no attempt at shaping. (See Figure 1.) The arms are similarly vestigial. While a few have glass eyes, most of them have painted eyes, formed

of a round black dot enclosed by two thin lines in almond shape with a third line for the brow which almost meets its opposite.

One of the dolls in nearly pristine condition is in the collection of Mrs. Earle E. Andrews. When parts of the original costume remain on these dolls they agree on being Empire or Directoire, dating them about 1795 to 1815. The overskirt is a gauzy material, often with a self pattern woven in at the bottom, and the underskirt is of stiff paper thus enabling it to stand. The legs do not come nearly to the bottom of the skirt.

These dolls were at first quite a puzzle to us for, while primitive looking, they had well-shaped noses which implied considerable carving. And yet every other feature indicated an attempt to produce the doll with as little effort and as cheaply as possible. The puzzle unravelled slowly. In Philadelphia, Pennsylvania, Mrs. Walton showed us one of these dolls with a vertical crack down each side of the face. Did we know of any reason why these cracks should develop?

Thus alerted, the answer turned up in the home George Washington bought for his mother, now maintained as a museum in Fredericksburg, Virginia. The custodian kindly let us examine a doll with a cracked face in one of the cases, and the fracture disclosed the secret. It proved to be one of this type with glass eyes and the face,

Figure 1.

Illustration 25. Head of an English wooden doll with flax hair, glass eyes, and dotted eyebrows. The wooden body is jointed at the arms and legs. Late 18th century. 27in (69cm) tall.

BELOW: Illustration 26: Early 20th century German peg-wooden dolls, 10in (25cm), 7in (18cm) and 3½in (9cm) tall. Last of the line. Carved wood head 4½in (12cm) high. 19th century.

Illustration 27: Three seated German wooden lady dolls with wire jointing. Original ethnic clothes. Center hair style dates to 1840, the others to 1830. 13in (33cm) tall.

which had separated from the flat front of the wooden head, was now seen to be cast in plaster.

Later we purchased one of these dolls from Mrs. Lee Weadon. In our dryer climate, the wood has now shrunk away from the plaster head so that it can be moved. Another example in rather good condition (except the paper underskirt of its original costume is bent and crumpled) is in the Toy Shop of the Henry Ford Museum in Dearborn, Michigan. Two well used specimens with remnants of their original Empire clothing are in the Children's Museum in Boston, Massachusetts. Mrs. Helen Hinckley had several good ones which have been re-costumed. One of these dolls, now at Colonial Williamsburg, is from the family of President Tyler.

And so these plaster-faced, painted-eye, pointed-torso, small wooden dolls mark the end of one lineage of doll making in England. This lineage, its simple beginnings practically lost to us, produced its finest examples, now of great rarity, during the William and Mary period, probably sustained through the reign of Queen Anne. Conventionalization accompanying mass production marked the decline in craftsmanship during the reigns of the first two Georges, and the final fall came with the fourth of the Georges.

While we were doing the research of correcting conjectures we became concerned with a large group of wax mannequins which are in both private and museum collections. Our own specimens shown in Illustrations 20

and 21, have solid cast wax heads and wax arms. They are elaborately costumed in the style of the Empire Period. They are one of a half-dozen selected by the late George Ertell from a large group in a Paris collection. The costumes ranged from the 17th century to 1850. The heads are cast in one piece with the shoulders and breast, while the rest of the body is cloth wrapped on a wire armature. This type of figure stimulated a series of conjectures and refutations.

Conjecture No. 1 for us was that this was a mannequin of the period denoted by her costume; in our case Empire. The wax on ours was very dark, implying considerable age. The close similarity of face and hands to those in other collections might be accounted for as being a traditional form persisting over many years. There is a pair in the Museum of the City of New York which the donor described as fashion dolls used before the day of the colored fashion plate. This implied that each was dressed at the time of its style.

But there were doubts; a mannequin can, of course, be dressed in any style previous to the date it was dressed. We next saw a group of a dozen or so in the collection of Madame de Galéa in Paris. She said they were of the period of Napoleon III (mid 19th century) — that is, at the time of the latest costume of the group. So we switched to conjecture No. 2, that a large number of these mannequins had been made at mid-century for a display of the history of costume.

NOTRE CONCOURS DE POUPÉES HABILLÉES

(Pl. Lumière.)   POUPÉES "MIGNONNETTES".

NOTRE Concours de Poupées habillées a été clôturé par une Exposi-ion des plus réussies, qui a duré du 15 au 25 octobre à *Femina*. Le jury fut fort embar-rassé pour distribuer les récom-penses: deux prix et huit souvenirs. Tout d'a-bord, il mit hors concours, en raison de nombreuses récompenses déjà conquises, les poupées de *Mmes Lafitte-Daussat* (de Paris), qui exposèrent des danseuses harmonieuses souples et vivantes. C'est à *Mlle Riera* (de Paris) que revient le PRE-MIER PRIX (un bijou d'une valeur de 300 francs). *Mmes Jungbluth et Soulié* (de Paris) se partagent le SECOND PRIX (un bijou d'une valeur de 150 francs.) Quant aux huit souvenirs, ils ont été décernés à *Mmes Pillois, Saratoff, Natanelli, Leroy, Litang, Derauro, Baussmann, Delong.*

SIMONE D'AX.

BOIARD RUSSE, PAR Mlle SARATOFF.

BOIARD RUSSE. PAR Mlle SARATOFF.

POUPÉES DE Mlle RIERA (Premier prix).
Bouquetière Louis XV, Mariée second Empire et la " Femme au manchon", trois poupées exquises de grâce délicate et fine.

POUPÉES DE Mme JUNGBLUTH (2e prix).
Reconstitution parfaite des modes du second Empire et 1830.

POUPÉES DE Mme LAFITTE-DAUSSAT (Hors concours).
Trois danseuses d'une fantaisie étourdissante, d'une vie intense et d'une vérité d'attitude inimitable.

Alsacienne en costume national.

GARDEN-PARTY PAR Mme SOULIÉ (2e prix).
Figurée par des poupées habillées de papier, de silhouette ultra-moderne.

Nourrice berrichonne.

494

Figure 2.

58

There the matter rested until we saw the cover picture of the August 1964 *Doll News*. Here was the same vague little hand, the same black bead eyes, and the same type of face with uptilted chin and long neck. It was said to be a portrait of Marie Antoinette sculptured in the 18th century. But the figure did not speak to us convincingly of the Louis XVI court. Where was the clean-cut line of the stomacher, and why was the hair brought down around the face instead of being brushed up high from the forehead and back to low curls at the side?

We started further inquiries. We found that the Merritt Doll Museum had acquired a group of thirty-three of these mannequins. On a postcard showing three of these dolls it said: "...in original costumes (circa 1490-1850)." This is the same as our conjecture No. 1. However, they also have a museum brochure (text by Ann Kilborn Cole) which says on page 17: "A shelf of French Wax dolls made about 1850 and probably fashioned for display are dressed in period styles dating from a costume of the late 1600s to the year in which they were made." This agrees with our conjecture No. 2. (When we later saw these figures we noted they had faded labels all in the same handwriting, indicating a common time of assembling.)

An inquiry to John Noble, Curator of the Toy Department of The Museum of the City of New York, brought forth some very upsetting ideas leading into conjecture No. 3. We quote:

"On the subject of the wax costume dolls I can be more positive. I have again examined the group of them in our costume collection, and confirmed my earlier conclusions, that they are part of a series illustrating the history of costume, and that they were made between 1900 and 1910.

"It is a fact that, however earnest one's wish for accuracy, one can only see the costumes of the past with the eye of one's own time, and any attempted reconstruction of these costumes will always betray the era in which they themselves were made. Try as we may, there is a blind spot in the recent past, when the styles seem ugly and incomprehensible, and there will be other periods which seem to be in harmony with our own tastes....

"These wax figures give many clues to their date of fabrication; the over-sweetness of posture and gesture, for instance, quite unlike the elegance and restraint of the 18th century waxes, or the curious self certainty of the Victorian ones. Then the over-rich, over-heavy fabrics in muted 'art' colors and fussy dowdy-genteel trimmings, which are used on all the figures regardless of period, are in the taste of 1900. The hairstyles, too, of the dolls that I examined, and apparently of Mrs. Merritt's dolls, are period hairstyles interpreted by 1900-1910 taste....

"Such sets of figures seem to have been popular at this time. I am enclosing a page from a French magazine, *Femina*, dated November 1, 1908 (see Figure 2). The dolls of Madame Jungbluth show distinct similarities of genre with the dolls we are discussing. It is significant that, at this exposition, there is an emphasis of dolls as 'art' figurines, rather than as playdolls. I am also enclosing two clippings from the same issue, both with the same stylistic character of the head of the doll on the extreme right of the Merritt postcard."

We have recently found John Noble's considerations reinforced in a book by Otto Kurz, titled *Fakes*. From page 317 of the 1967 Dover edition we quote: "But even the most adaptable talent, the most perfect imitator, has his own distinctive inflection and, above all, his is a child of his own time. Every forgery will, unconsciously, show symptoms of the style of the epoch which produced it. Contemporaries may not discern it, but from a distance, the signs of the true period of origin gradually become apparent. Friedlander once said that the life of a forgery does not outlast thirty years, in other words, its own generation."

While these mannequins were not intended as forgeries to deceive anyone at the time of their creation the same principles apply, and it is not surprising that an experienced curator like John Noble has called this to our attention after two generations.

By a fortunate coincidence, the souvenir book of the Washington UFDC convention at which we presented a workshop on research, reprinted on pp. 20-21 an article "Dolls That Illustrate History," taken from the *Delineator* for December 1912. It tells of the work of Mademoiselle Riera in the making of similar historical costume creations using ceramic-headed mannequins.

The page from *Femina* reports the prizes awarded at an exposition of dressed dolls or rather, as John Noble pointed out, "art" figurines. These entries are the product of an adult hobby. Across the top is a row of "Mignonettes," tiny dolls dressed in fanciful costumes, flanked by two large dolls dressed in Russian costumes. The group of three just below are the entry of Madamoiselle Riera whose work was described in the *Delineator* article: a Louis IV flower girl, a bride of the second Empire, and woman with muff. She was awarded a first prize. Of the next row of seven the four at the left were the entry of Madame Jungbluth, mentioned by John Noble as being of the wax mannequin type we are discussing. They are reported as 1830 and second Empire (1850) and won second prize. The other three represented dancers of the day. The two large dolls at the bottom displayed provincial costumes, and the center group were dolls dressed in paper with "Silhouette ultra-modern." (Figure 2.)

The bead-eyed wax mannequin thus appears to be but one phase of an adult hobby or fad for historical costuming participated in by professionals and amateurs during the first quarter of the 20th century. This may also provide an explanation of why these figures have turned up in sizeable groups; first that collectors would assemble sets of the work of their favorite "artist" just as many now collect the work of present day "doll artists," such as Martha Thompson or Dorothy Heiser; and second, such hobbyists would accumulate a large number of their own making which in due time would be passed along in the family. It further accounts for the variation in craftsmanship.

For some it became more than a hobby, it was a source of income. In a recent conversation with Mrs. W. Lee Weadon, a former director of the Doll Collectors of America, she told us that about 1925 she purchased wax mannequins of this type from Paris which were named after noted persons: Marie Antoinette, Empress Josephine, or Empress Eugenie, and so on. Whether dressed commercially or by a hobbyist, it is highly probable that some well-known portrait of the subject was used as a guide for copying. Thus in a modern series displaying the inaugural or other gowns of the first ladies of the White House, the Smithsonian book on these costumes may have been a guide.

Two other clippings referred to by John Noble illustrate hat and hair styles of the first decade of the 20th century. They also illustrate the popular ideal of feminine beauty of the day further celebrated by such artists as Charles Dana Gibson and Harrison Fisher. (Figure 4.)

The facial style of these wax mannequins fits the period. If one goes back to the mid-Victorian days one finds a similar congruence of portraits, fashion plated and doll faces. Most of the so-called portrait dolls, like the Jenny Lind, are simply the result of the toy world keeping in step with the adult world of style.

We compare our Empire costumed mannequin (Illustration 21) with two other figures. These illustrate side ramifications of the fad similar to those on the page from *Femina*. In the one at the right the eyes are not beads but molded in the wax and surface painted. The hands are more detailed. A faded label on the base states it represents Sarah Bernhardt (color photo on page 36) in the role "Lady of the Camellias." A rear view of Sarah is strikingly like the fashion of the left hand one of the three dancers in *Femina*. Part of Bernhardt's career was contemporary with the fad for these "art figurines." The lady with the mandolin (color photo on page 36) was a solid wax half-torso on a crude wood block for the lower half, solid wax arms jointed at the shoulder and wax legs to the hips. The hands are finely modeled with long slender fingers. All seem to tie in with the pattern described by John Noble.

These considerations lead us to state conjecture No. 3: the group of wax mannequins just described are to be regarded as the product of an adult fad of the first quarter of the 20th century. This we regard as a valid hypothesis unless, or until, new factual data should be found to refute it.

For a final example of the research process we wish to consider a case in which the source of our original data is a highly specialized art. Here we must be careful that incorrect conjectures are not made because of lack of understanding of that art. For this we have selected the patent art. We are fortunate that Mrs. Luella Hart has made available to us brief abstracts of patents relating to dolls of four countries; Germany, England, France, and the United States. Similar information is provided by the Colemans in *Dolls, Makers and Marks* and *The Age of Dolls*.

Those parts of these publications which list firms making or dealing in dolls, their addresses at certain dates, and more, offer a few problems in interpretation. However, in the case of patents there are pitfalls to be aware of. For example, we have seen it stated in the doll

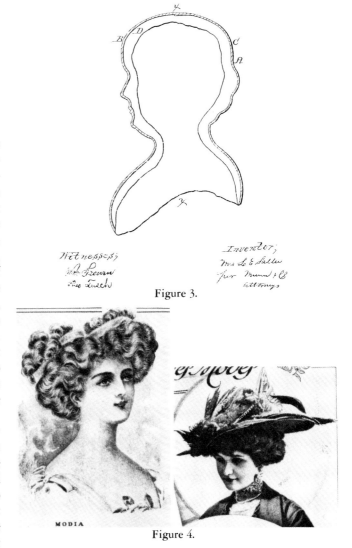

Figure 3.

Figure 4.

literature that an inventor must have manufactured his invention for sale before he could get a patent. (Probably a false analogy with a copyright which can be secured only after depositing two copies of the publication in the Library of Congress.) While this is incorrect, it is true that originally the United States patent laws required that the inventor submit a model of his invention. Figure 3 is such a model for a doll head. It was filed on December 24, 1864, and issued on February 7, 1865, only one and a half months later. With the complete model of the head were also filed samples of the materials used — leather, paper, and glue. The patent number is 46,270. We have no information that this doll was ever made commercially. The inventor was Lucretia E. Sallee. We also have a pair of such patent models for the Weigand doll showing two stages of manufacture. It is patent, No. 177,777, issued on May 23, 1876, made commercially. They now reside in the Strong Museum in Rochester, New York.

Later, in 1880, because of storage problems, the law was changed to require only a written description which would enable those "skilled in the art" to apply the invention. It is the interpretation of this standardized written description which is subject to certain pitfalls. To be valid the invention must be new and useful. The text begins with stating the objective of the invention, the new idea for solving a problem. The body of the patent describes in detail how the new idea may be applied in specific cases. The last part of the patent consists of a list of claims.

In drawing these claims the patent lawyer will try to make the scope of the idea as broad as possible. Together with the inventor he will list every possible use they can imagine. This practice of multiple claiming can be the prime factor in leading some to arrive at wrong conjectures and conclusions. It may easily lead to two kinds of error: First, that what is claimed as two different things are assumed to be one and the same. Second, that an article manufactured is regarded as being a fulfillment of another claim. This is the explanation, but not the excuse for the erroneous popular misnomer, "Milliner's Models."

First we wish to question a conclusion drawn from a French process patent issued to Soret in 1847. On page 92 of Luella Hart's *French Doll Directory* this process is described as: "System of making papier-mâché heads for baby dolls and for milliners and hairdressers." In Cole-

man's *Dolls, Makers and Marks* on page 68, this phrase is translated: "....papier-mâché heads for babes and for 'modiste' model dolls." In both cases the conjunction between the two uses is "and" and not "or." This indicates two separate uses. In fact, at this time large papier-mâché heads were in common use to display wigs and hats. This view is further supported by the listing for the years 1833 and 1839 (pp. 2-4 of Hart's *French Directory*) of Cochet-Verdey as "makers of dolls in papier-mâché or kid and heads for milliners and hairdressers." These are two separate products although both could have been made by the same process. The fact that both were claimed eight years later as items which could be made by his process does not make them the same.

We therefore cannot agree with the statement made on p. 92 of the *French Directory* under Patent No. 5198: "This patent is one of three that prove there were doll heads made called milliner's models used by milliners and drapers." Papier-mâché heads? Yes. But doll heads? No.

Illustration 28: Miniature peg-woodens, all under 1in (3cm) tall. Smallest dolls in locket are the earliest. Germany.

There are other independent and cogent reasons for disagreeing with St. George's use of the term "Milliner's Models" for the doll, a child's toy of that period.

No patent is regarded as valid until it has been tested in court for both operability and originality. The United States Patent Office has a competent staff of examiners who do much to assure the patent's validity before it is issued. However, the French do not. There, the word for patented, "Brevete," must be accompanied by the letters S.D.G.D., standing for a phrase meaning, "Without guarantee of government." Thus the issuing of a patent does little more than establish a date of registering an idea. It is likely that a reasonable search would have denied a patent to Soret. His idea was to replace molding with a pulp of mashed paper by laying successive layers of thin paper with adhesive inside of a mold or a matrix. Jane Teller, in the book *Papier-mâché in England and America* (1962) reports that Obediah Westwood patented this process in 1792. Basically the general process is very old; the Egyptians made mummy cases from papyrus in this way.

Incidentally, material made by this process should have a definition in the U.F.D.C. *Glossary* of terms. We would suggest "laminar papier-mâché" or more simply, "laminar papier." In the August 1965 *Doll News* Liba Benton discussed the use of this material in doll bodies and suggests the term "matrix." However, "matrix" is defined as a "mold" which normally is used with either the pulp or the layering process.

Because of the French procedures we may well expect more troubles in the case of French patents. Indeed, our second pitfall is illustrated by another French patent issued to Benoit Martin on March 3, 1863. On the cover of Hart's *French Directory* is a photograph of a very fine doll. Below the correct title, "BENOIT MARTIN DOLL," there is the statement: "This is an artist's mannequin." With this we would disagree. Martin claims that his improved hip joint will provide a figure which can hold a sitting position. This he says was not previously possible. A glance at Illustration 3 shows that the classic artist's model, used since the time of Durer in the 16th century can sit very well. Furthermore, this figure with its joints at the neck, midriff, shoulders, elbows, wrists, hips, knees and ankles, fourteen in all, can assume a greater variety of positions than the Martin doll with its hip joint moveable in only one plane. Some of the larger of these figures were so completely articulated as to include the fingers and the toe joints. The special type of jointing, ball and socket, allowed a wide angle of adjustment with ease and yet had sufficient friction to hold almost any pose.

Now obviously Martin followed his patent in making a very fine doll. The fact that Martin also claimed his patent could be used for making a better artist's model does not justify calling this "doll" an "artist's mannequin." That is, an embodiment of one claim of a patent is not to be taken as a realization of another alternate claim directed to another use. For an artist to try using a Martin doll as a guide to patterns of composition of the human figure would be most distracting because of the varied materials and colors. All artist's models we know of are left in the natural wood finish. (Except in those cases where one has been diverted from its original purpose and converted into a character as a priest or Abraham Lincoln. We have seen two Abraham Lincolns and one on

Illustrations 29A and 29B: Head of a peg-wooden doll (front and back views) with elaborately styled floss wig. c.1830.

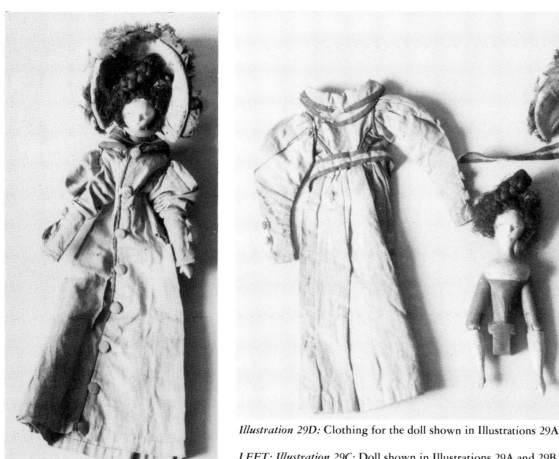

Illustration 29D: Clothing for the doll shown in Illustrations 29A, 29B and 29C.

LEFT: Illustration 29C: Doll shown in Illustrations 29A and 29B dressed.

which a most interesting wax head was formed; a semi-bald man with inserted grey hair.) The only reason we can imagine for an artist using a Martin doll as a model would be to paint a picture of a Martin doll. Are there any records of the "doll" being advertised for sale to artists? The fact that there is an issued patent with these claims means nothing, for the brass plate on the doll carries the standard mark, "Brevete, S.G.D.G." — "without guarantee of the government."

That we encounter these difficulties in the interpretation of patents does not mean that patents are of no importance in our study of the development of the doll. They provide valuable data on dates, business competition, the relationship between various arts and technologies, and much more. However, the material in them should be regarded very critically and verified by other sources of information. The text may often be an expression of wishful thinking and not an accomplished fact. Probably a majority of patents are paper patents — that is, they have never been used. Reliance for final conclusions should not be based on brief abstracts and idioms of the time.

We would like to suggest the following rule be followed in studying patents: Never regard the material in a patent as a statement of fact, but only as establishing the date of an idea (original or otherwise) and a clue to a possibility, the existence and final character of which must be determined by independent evidence. Very often a patent is a statement of an inventor's hopes, not of his accomplishments.

From our research of the wax mannequins we can return to the peg-woodens after popular interest in the English Woodens faded.

A new tribe of dolls was invading the industry; dolls with prettier faces, with better-proportioned bodies and with the multiple jointing system. As they were largely the product of peasants, made during the long winters or in the evenings, they could be made more cheaply than in an industrial society. While dolls of the character similar to the Queen Anne type as equally crude were being made in many Continental countries, this new form seems to have originated in a very definite region.

Back of the story of the peg-woodens lies primarily that of the artist's lay figure as well as the sacred image. von Boehn in Chap. VII of *Dolls and Puppets* traces these mannequins back in literature to the 15th century and

discusses them and the artists who used them.

In Illustrations 22A and 22B we see the fine jointing, described in relationship to Illustration 3, carried over into religious figures. This Tobias and the Angel have all the jointing system of the artist's model except the midriff, ankle, and wrist.

However, the taller figure has the lower part of the forearm rotatable with respect to the upper. The face, hands, and feet are carved with a high degree of realism (the Angels ankles are lean; the child's chubby) and are finished with varnish enamel. The bodies are carved with partial realism and left unpainted. These figures would appear to be 18th century or possibly late 17th.

During the 18th century excellent wood sculpture was also applied to many secular figures and puppets. The color photo on page 76 shows a pair of heads similar to those in Johl's *The Fascinating Story of Dolls*, page 46. The horizontal curls carved in the wood were a popular Louis XVI style. The figures of these heads are very loose jointed, similar to puppets, but puppets for public showing were carved with features extra large and strong to carry visually to an audience.

We note, therefore, a rich background of craftsmanship out of which toy and doll makers could draw their inspiration. Just where this crystallized into a continuing industry is a point about which there has been much controversy, and which cannot as yet be fully resolved. As regards the peg-woodens we can only suggest what we at present believe the most likely history.

The distinctive type of doll was most generally called "Dutch dolls" by the English, and "Nuremberg filles" by the French. Many maintain that these names in themselves tell the story; obviously they say the origins were Holland and Nuremberg, Germany. But this does not seem to stand up well upon investigation. The British have a habit of using a point of purchase for a name. Thus dolls bought at the Bartholomew Fair became "Bartholomews babies" no matter where made. Likewise, dolls bought from the wholesalers at the great fairs at Bruge, Belgium, and Nuremberg, Germany, became "Flanders babies" or "Dutch dolls" (with Dutch as a corruption of Deutsch.) We have seen no record of a community in the Low Countries with an early history of wooden dolls being an important local industry. Mrs. R. C. Williams reported writing repeatedly to official agencies in Holland with no results. She also cited a book of the 1880s, *The Wonderland of Work*, by C. L. Mateaux, as saying, "The Dutch dolls which, by the way, never came from Holland at all...." Though there are records of Nuremberg, Germany, having doll makers who worked in plastic materials, such as clay, pulp, or gum tragacanth, the city served chiefly as a wholesaling center with no real part in the production of wooden toys, as will be developed further.

While the above two names will always be with us in the history of these dolls, it now seems preferable to drop them from present day nomenclature because of their incorrect connotation as to point of origin. The term penny wooden is romantically attractive but actually applied only to the smaller sizes and is tied to the currency of the nation, not where they originated, but where they had the most enthusiastic reception. Other terms, like German pipestems, double-jointed doll, wooden Betty, and others, are too localized. Stick doll applies more appropriately to the poupard and swaddled babe. Key point in the construction of these dolls, whether made with the ball and socket joint, or the cruder mortise and tenon, is the use of tiny wooden pegs for the final articulation. A concise and descriptive term which we would therefore recommend is "peg-wooden."

The first published summary in this country pointing to the probable point of origin of the peg-woodens as being the Grödner Tal was provided by Miss Jennie Abbott (for many years historian of the Doll Collectors of America) in the 1946 issue of the *Manual* under the title of "Penny Woodens." Her source material included von Boehn, Karl Grober, Baedecker, and Baillie-Grahams's book on the Tyrol. Later, Mrs. R. C. Williams (Darcy), after an extensive study came to the same conclusion. Unfortunately, most of her source material has been lost.

As so many doll books, including von Boehn, say or imply that practically indistinguishable forms of the peg-wooden were carved over a wide area from the forests of Thuringia in Bohemia and at several points in the Bavarian and Austrian Alps, it is desirous to review how this idea began and why it might be incorrect.

The best background we have in English is provided by the translation of Karl Grober's book, *Children's Toys of Bygone Days*. He deals with toys broadly and emphasizes that toys were a by-product of the regular work of the craft guilds. He quotes Christoph Weigel in 1698: "Indeed there is scarce a trade in which that which is usually made big may not often be seen copied on a small scale as a toy for playing with." The toys were shipped along with consignments of the larger articles. Each guild had to call in the help of other crafts for what was outside their own field. For this reason only the most elaborate forms of toys were made in the cities, as they could not compete with the cheaper toys of the outlying wood-carving districts.

Grober cites the four major wooden toy producers as Sonneberg (in Thuringia to the north of Nuremberg) and Oberammergau, Berchtesgaden, and the Grödner Tal in the Bavarian and Austrian Tyrol to the southeast of Nuremberg. These areas developed their woodcarving during the 17th and 18th centuries. At first these areas marketed their toys through pedlars and independent agents, but about the beginning of the 19th century wholesale houses dealing only in toys became established in Nuremberg, which became the toy distributing center of the world. Thus many toys were ascribed to Nuremberg that were never made there.

Grober also describes the case of a group of wood-carvers who, for religious reasons, left Berchtesgaden, Germany, about 1735 and tried to establish their business near Nuremberg. In spite of the backing of the Nuremberg dealers, the project failed. Hence this city should be regarded not as a maker but as a distributor of wooden dolls, and we must look to one of the peasant craft areas mentioned above for the source of the jointed doll.

Unfortunately Grober does not have a single illustration of a peg-wooden doll in his profusely illustrated book. We can, however, draw a few inferences from what he does show. The facial characteristics of the small figures from Sonneberg, Germany, are so different from those of the peg-wooden that it seems the least likely source. Of the three Alpine areas the toys of Berchtesgaden show the least stylistic resemblance to the peg-woodens.

The closest resemblance of those shown in Grober's plates are numbers 161 and 163 of Oberammergau — the former of seven swaddling babes, and the latter a score of shoulder head woodens. Plate 162 is of a group of 18 jumping-jacks with joints of a very different type. He states the Langsches Museum has a very complete series of examples of the work in that area so why did he not have a corresponding plate of peg-wooden dolls? Our guess would be because they were the product principally of the neighboring Grödner Tal, while the stylistic similarity would be due to the fact that, as told by Grober, in the earliest days the Grödners did not have the art of painting and had to send their dolls to Oberammergau to be painted.

Now as to more positive evidence pointing to the Grödner Tal. von Boehn in his *Dolls and Puppets* shows in Figure 120 a peg-wooden of early romantic hair style which is in the Spielzeug Museum at Sonneberg, Germany, and is there credited to the Grödner Tal. The head of this doll shows a characteristic quite common to the early peg-woodens; the features are relatively small and concentrated on the lower half of the face with an overly high forehead. One of the most fascinating is a wooden walking doll in the collection of Mr. and Mrs. Jesse Bottomley which advances on a rotating rimless wheel of eight legs. Examination of the photo and notes on page 54 of the 1956-57 *Manual* shows that the torso and head are very like the English Woodens, while the feet and arms are quite similar to the peg-woodens.

Another one-of-a-kind doll from the Bottomley collection has the fully developed set of eight ball and socket peg-wooden joints. The unusual feature is that the breasts are well defined. This would indicate that the doll was made about the end of the 18th century when the gowns assumed a very low decolletage. The jointing suggests it was a doll. For a mannequin figure to display such a dress, full jointing was not necessary. This image was called pregnant doll by the dealer from whom we obtained it, and by many collectors who see it. However, reference to paintings of the nudes of that period indicates it was simply the normal uncorseted figure of those days. (The French contemporaneously ridiculed the "long corset" of the English. See Figure 2295, page 818, Davenport's *Book of Costume*.)

While the basic dependence of the peg-wooden on the artist's model for its inspiration is fairly obvious from the standard eight ball and socket joints found on the larger sizes at the turn of the century, this hypothesis is made still more certain by noting the number of dolls in the larger sizes (20 to 22in [51 to 56cm]) which also have the midriff joint. There is a fine example in the Chester County Historical Society, West Chester, Pennsylvania. A

similar fine doll of this period belongs to Mrs. E. H. Poetter. It has a midriff joint, elaborate comb and a carved yoke decorated in red and gold. This doll was shown dressed on the cover of *Doll News* for August 1961.

There is little to tie one of these earliest figures to the Grödner Tal except for general considerations fitting well into the overall pattern. von Boehn tells us that artist's models were made in large sizes for several centuries before the peg-wooden doll. Because of their small numbers and excellent proportioning we may assume they were made to special order by master craftsmen of the city guilds. The pathway of art, from the Renaissance in northern Italy to central Europe, was via the Brenner Pass not far from St. Ulrich in the Grödner Tal. (St. Ulrich is now a chief tourist center for the Dolomites in northern Italy.) We also know from Miss Howitt that the Grodners were carving religious images in the early 1700s. However, the demand for such images was falling off due to the spread of Protestantism in northern Europe. What then was more natural than that the Grödners seized upon the familiar artist's model to exploit as a toy and expand their line of goods. Popularity in sales then decided the specific form to make in quantity. This they did in a range of sizes from one half inch (1cm) to two feet (61cm) from the early 19th century to fairly recent days. We have not yet been able to determine whether those sold now are old stock or whether some are still being made.

Also, for these odd variations, the relative dating of some of these figures is uncertain. Fortunately, however, for what we may call the classic form of the peg-woodens, there was a series of changes in hair style and body shapes with which the doll makers followed, in spirit, the rapidly shifting patterns of women's fashions in those days. This provides for approximate dating over an important period. With the French Revolution, wigs were discarded revealing hair which had been cut short. At the same time, as part of the Greek revival spirit, not only were political ideas adopted but high-waisted loose gowns. Both are clearly shown in Illustration 17 — (right) a wind-blown bob or pixie hair style and the Greek style of dress. It thus appears safe to place this doll as mid-1790s.

A few early dolls are known which are above the usual maximum of about 22in (56cm) in height; there is such a doll in the West Chester Historical Society, in extra fine condition and with a family history. The loose locks fringing the forehead and the Directoire costume place it close to 1800. The features are strongly carved and it has a carved yoke line with the breasts partially exposed. Another such doll, 28½in (72cm), of the same period is in the collection of Dorothy Dixon, Vista, California. It is even more pixie-like with its scraggly hair style. The upper arms and torso from waist to knees have been covered with white kid. Over the buttocks the leather has been padded out to give a more shapely derriere, so it may have been used as a dressmaker's mannequin. Both these larger dolls have been done in an individual style as to head and hands, though the bodies have the typical eight ball and socket joints. A third high-waisted doll of the 29in (74cm) size is in the collection of Mrs. Lee Weadon. It was distinguished by having a decorated comb, and also by having the midriff joint.

Dolls within the one to two feet (31 to 61cm) size range also turn up with variations which indicate luxury appeal, or perhaps special order. One such doll, now in the Society for the Preservation of New England Antiquities, Otis House, Boston, Massachusetts, is designed to be provided with a wig. The low waistline places this figure between 1825 and 1840.

But of all the peg-woodens we know, the most aristocratic is at the Santa Barbara (California) Museum of Art in the Alice F. Schott collection. Thirty-nine inches (99cm) tall, she has an elaborately carved and decorated yoke, painted in tints reminiscent of those used at Oberammergau on swaddled babes and strongly suggestive of embroidery. The carved coiled braid stands partly free of the head on one side. A similar coil-braid style is shown in Figure 2294 on page 818 of Davenport's *Book of Costume*. This is a painting of Marie Louise of Austria taking leave of her family. The museum label on this doll says it came from Vienna, Austria, probably the home of the princess for whom it was made to special order. And where should such a special order be placed but in one of the wood carving areas which was in Austria — the Grödner Tal? Or it may have been a gift to the Court of their Empire by the Grödners.

In general, the period of finest quality in carving and translucence of enamel is associated with the last decade of the 18th century and the first two of the 19th century, as in Illustration 17. Combs appeared with the Empire

Illustration 30: All wood doll of the Empire period with unique pregnant body. 19th century. 16½in (42cm) tall.

period and continued into the third decade when quality was beginning to deteriorate.

The very popularity of the peg-wooden led to its downfall. It developed a mass market, and with the mass market came mass production methods and, more serious, there came competition. While we have not made an extensive study of papier-mâché doll heads we have noted early forms with short curly hair coming low on the forehead. One of these was on a stiff kid body shaped to a definitely high waistline. Two others had been used on dolls' house dolls dressed as men. They had been put on peg-wooden dolls whose heads had been cut off, apparently to fit the Directoire style. When men's hair became stylishly longer in the Empire or early Romantic period, these dolls were brought up-to-date by the sewing on of floss wigs. This indicates that in the very popular 6 to 7in (15 to 18cm) dolls' house size competition was active from papier-mâché heads by 1800-1810.

While many of the dolls dressed about 1825-1830 had combs, it is already evident that the quality of the carving was then markedly less fine than around the turn of the century. The best available photo reproductions of her dolls are in Mrs. Early's *English Dolls, Effigies and Puppets*, plates 27 through 32. Less useful are those in an article by Francis H. Low in the *Strand* magazine in 1892, pages 223-238. This article was converted into a book in 1894, *Queen Victoria's Dolls*, in which delicate watercolors have prettified the dolls almost beyond recognition. In Illustration 4 are a pair of dolls contemporary with the Countess of Jedburgh and the Duchess of Orleans of the book. The one wearing the hat has no comb. The one with the comb, also wearing a hat, has a peak shown on the forehead leading to a part in the hairdo which, together with the spit curls, identifies these dolls as late Empire or early romantic (the dress style being 1830). When the doll still has loose bangs on the forehead (holding over from the pixie cut) together with spit curls at the side, it may be placed in the first decade of the 19th century.

By 1830-1840 the comb was being omitted and the waist line was lowered. In the largest sizes, 22in (56cm), all eight joints were still ball and socket and there was still often very fine carving. The type of finish also changed during the early decades of the 19th century. Instead of the deep translucent effect secured by clear varnish over watercolor, it becomes an enamel — that is, a varnish with a tint in it.

Developing markets aroused new forms of competition. The making of these all-wooden peasant crafted dolls had in all probability spread to other areas. In the Folk Art Museum in Santa Fe, New Mexico, is a pair of a type of peg-woodens which are very elongated, and Mrs. R. H. Walton of Philadelphia, Pennsylvania, has a similar pair which Mrs. R. C. Williams identified as being from Oberammergau, Germany. However, we do not know the specific basis for this identification.

Bohemia has also developed some distinctive forms of all the wooden dolls with the torsos painted in bright colors. Plate 33 in Hercik's book, *Folk Toys — Les Jouet Populaire* (Orbis, Prague, 1952), shows a doll with ball and socket joints similar to the Tyrolean; a blue-bodied doll with peg joints rather different and a red-bodied doll (Illustration 16) with kid or cloth joints. While we have never seen the one with the blue body we have seen quite

a few with the red torso. It was made in a number of sizes and on the larger ones, 20 to 24in (51 to 61cm) tall, more elaborate hair styles were carved. Mrs. Earle E. Andrews had a fine example with unusual yellow hair carved in the 1840 style and falling low over the ears with a knot at the back.

As the peg-wooden idea was spreading through central Europe, a quite different approach was developed. Grober has pointed out that it was the custom of the Nuremberg wholesalers to send samples of popular items to various toymakers to get competitive bids for lower prices. Carving charming little faces on these wooden bodies took skill and time even though the features were becoming more conventionalized under the normal pressure of quantity production.

Artisans who were familiar with molding plaster, clay, and pulps now proceeded to mold heads for all these wooden bodies. We have seen a man's china head on a peg body. Here the hands and feet are also of china. The hair style of those we have seen fall into a period of about 1836 to 1860. While they are found mostly in the five and six inch (13 and 15cm) size, they were made up to 20in (51cm) tall as shown in the fine example in the collection of Mrs. Orrel M. Andrews, St. Joseph, Missouri. This shoulder head is pegged in place. There is only one peg in the rear center as both back corners are cut away to provide space for putting in the shoulder joint pegs, thus showing that these heads were made especially to go on peg-wooden bodies. Another form of china head was solid except for a central vertical hole so the head could be slipped over a cylindrical projection from the shoulders.

The third type of molded head is often not recognized as being anything other than an all wooden head — even by collectors with long experience in collecting wooden dolls. This is a plaster head molded solidly over a peg projecting from the shoulders. They were made in two general forms — (1) bald headed, and (2) bonnet or hairdo types. The bald head has a smooth round head with a plain black cap painted on, giving no indication of hair style. They were to be fitted with wigs. The second kind may have hairdos, caps, coronets or bonnets molded integral with the head and sometimes gaily colored. Both types have the forearms and calves more smoothly turned than the usual peg-wooden. In addition, the few bald heads we have seen have had painted on a ribbon lacing

Illustration 31: Three wooden heads. The center head, 7in (18cm) tall, was found in the walls of the 16th century house being dismantled. 18th century. The two side heads, both 6½in (17cm) tall, are of the 19th century.

Illustration 32: Three Swiss jointed wooden dolls and one shoulder head, showing four different hair styles. All carved by a Swiss family who made them for generations. Early 20th century. Dolls are 10½in (27cm) tall.

Illustration 33: Javanese rod puppet (head close-up).

spiraling up around the calves to a bow, tied just under the knees.

We have seen a few examples of a rare variant in which the face and head are of wood but a somewhat elaborate coronet hairstyle, with a comb indicated at the back of the head added in plaster. These are referred to as the Empress Josephine hairdo. We have seen examples in the collections of Imogene Anderson, Lydia Bowerman, and Marjorie Siebert. Mr. George Ertwell also sent us a color slide of one of these as a shoulder type head on a cotton body. Whether these came from the same area as the previous types, we do not know. They may simply be an example of the larger size dolls of a series being made more elaborately, as they are dolls of the 10 to 12in (25 to 31cm) size, while the other two types we have seen only in 3 to 7in (8 to 18cm) size.

Mrs. R. C. Williams suggested an excellent term for these dolls with molded heads on wooden bodies — "alien heads." The fact that they are at present rarer than the all-woodens is probably because they are so much more fragile. When dolls were handled with more care for other reasons, as in the case of shell dolls used as decorative figures under glass, they have been preserved in relatively larger numbers.

While some form of hair style was generally carved on a shoulder type wooden head, this is seldom the case with the peg-wooden doll. When it is done, the angularity of the chisel marks reveals it. Hence, when a peg-wooden with a modeled hairdo or bonnet shows up, immediately suspect a plaster head. These also have a "softer" look and better formed mouth and eye sockets. We would estimate that these dolls were being made about 1830 to 1860, plus or minus. A group with gaily painted peasant bonnets came to us with some dolls' house material of the 1830-1840 period. As to where they were made we have no definite information. A clue is that many, perhaps a majority, of the shell dolls we have seen were of the plaster-head type. As a great many of the shell dolls were made along the coast from Normandy to Portugal, the nearest likely point of supply would be France, where the use of plaster and gesso had long been highly developed.

At all events, the molded head dolls had a devastating effect upon the peasant carvers in the Tyrol. Instead of accommodating themselves to using new techniques, they cheapened their all-wooden product. In a way, much

the same thing happened here as with the English Woodens under production pressure; the heads became less oval and more spherical and of the same diameter as the shoulders and hips, and the figure became dumpy, or should we say, a more Victorian shape.

From this time on, being in such a cheap class, little attention was paid to changing styles and they were made in much the same way until the end, except for getting cruder and being finished in paint instead of enamel. Noses were generally glued on. Later the feet were indicated by just a notch in the bottom of the leg and the two arms were no longer separately hinged at the shoulders, but to a stick running horizontally through the shoulders. The arms must now, perforce, move up and down together. Illustration 26 shows a group of these purchased from the Lanchester Marionettes.

The dolls in Illustration 26 have been an especial source of confusion. Roughly treated, left out in the rain and mud, many soon acquired a very antique appearance. When one lost its arms and legs and the home whittler carved a replacement, many assumed an even more primitive (and antique?) appearance. Time after time, we see photographs in antique and hobby magazines and on dealer's lists, labeled 18th century, and we try to correct the errors.

Another area of confusion lies in the ascription of many of these dolls (including English Woodens) to America. Americans, especially the Yankees, have had a great reputation for whittling. Hence, in the Index of American Design (National Gallery, Washington, D.C.) among the watercolors made by artists during the depression, one finds many such errors. Many of these watercolors are most commendable records of dress design, and so forth, of early days, but the notes with them, as a record of facts about the origin of the dolls, must be critically regarded.

In museums we have noted an English Wooden called Pennsylvania Dutch and another, painted black, a southern mammy. A peg-wooden with a comb has long been labeled Spanish, although the error has been repeatedly pointed out to the curator. Another jointed wooden doll with comb of the same size and type is in a folk art collection in a large art museum labeled, "Kentucky Stick Doll," and in another, "Cape Cod Doll." Hobbyists and craftsmen who do woodcarving say to us: "How can you

LEFT: *Illustration 34:* Two wax-over papier-mâché hatted dolls. Left: Home dressed doll. 19th century. 8in (20cm) tall. *Right:* All original 10½in (27cm) doll. Both made in Germany.

Illustration 35: Granny pedlar doll with wax head carrying a basket of collected items. England. 19th century. 8in (20cm) tall.

LEFT: *Illustration 36:* English wax doll of the Empire period (1820) with wire pull eyes. All original clothing.

be sure of that? Why anyone who is a good whittler can duplicate one of those crude dolls." To which we can only reply; "Yes, and No!" with the accent on the "No."

To appreciate this, consider the mid 19th century peg-wooden. When Mrs. R. C. Williams saw this doll in our collection, she said: "This looks like something I have been searching for. In a book on British industry I found a story stating that in the mid 19th century conditions were so bad that the London street pedlar could not afford to pay even the very low prices asked for the Tyrolean dolls. They made their day's stock in the evenings at home." Now, how does it differ from the continental doll? In both, the bodies have been turned on a lathe (probably a simple foot-treadle device). The arms and legs of the Tyrolean dolls are evidently pieces of dowel, made by driving a piece of wood through a round hole in a steel plate, a device used when large numbers of round rods are to be made quickly. The pedlar had no dowel-plate in this case, so he painfully whittled each arm and leg. He also attempted a little carving to bring out the nose of the face, a procedure long abandoned under mass production methods in the Tyrol. But the biggest give-away is in decorating the face — the lack of deftness, characteristic of one who has painted relatively few heads. The girl, reported by Margaret Howitt, who painted 100 dozen a week in her spare time, acquired a deftness that one learns to recognize almost as a trademark for those made in the Grödner Tal (the Val Gardena). One doll was found in New Jersey, so there is also the possibility that it may have been made by a pedlar in this country, as was the storybook doll, "Hitty." (They should not on this account be called pedlar dolls, a term already pre-empted for dolls equipped with trays of goods to represent street hawkers.)

The characteristic appearance of the Tyrolean dolls should enable the experienced collector to distinguish a number of copies from the peg-woodens made in this country. For example, after the supply of red bodies ran out at the House of Seven Gables in Salem, Massachusetts, they had at least two American whittlers make souvenir dolls for them. Even where the individual carvers makes quite a number of dolls, these differences in method and execution stand out. For example, the Holly Dolls of Ozone, Tennessee, or the delicately finished reproductions turned out by Sherman E. Smith of Midvale, Utah.

The great popularity of these Tyrolean peg-woodens

in England has led to a fairly frequent error, that of calling them English. Dressed in England, yes; made in England, no. In 1959 we saw an exceptionally fine group of these dolls, about twenty, in the Shelbourne (Vermont) Museum, all called English. Perhaps this love of the British children for these dolls has been best expressed in the article by Margaret Howitt: "Here are billions of wooden dolls, flung down helter-skelter, paid for by Herr Insam at five farthings the dozen, hereafter to be kissed, hugged, put to bed, rejoiced over by thousands of little English mothers. For it is in Great Britain, it seems, where most maternal instinct is shown in childhood, and these stiff wooden halfpenny dolls, exported often at the rate of 60 or 70 hundred-weight the week, become transformed on reaching England by the touch of love. Then these articles of trade turn into fairy princesses who perform pirouettes in a golden light on the branches of the ragged school Christmas trees. Then these items of debit and credit call forth the taste of some little dolls' dressmaker as she attires them in the latest Parisian fashion. These dolls marry and settle down when they reach England and dwell in houses, playing the piano, receiving visitors, instructing their children-puppets in the tiny fingers of juvenile providences who have placed them in these comfortable dolls' houses. How many of these cheap dolls become precious indeed; when lying on the pillows of children's hospital, they charm and sooth the little sufferers, so young to be tried in the furnace of affliction. Nearly all these myriads of dolls are for Great Britain. Those larger dolls' heads, it is true, are destined for Amsterdam, but they merely rest here bodies and the title, after which they resume their journey to become aunts and mothers to the lesser dolls which have already crossed the British Channel."

Illustration 31 shows three such shoulder type wooden doll heads; the smaller, a Tyrolean head, received from the Lanchester Marionettes, and the larger dates, perhaps, from just before the mid 19th century. The small head shows that here, just as in the case of the peg-woodens, when the doll became very cheap no attempt was made to follow the hair styles, instead a mid 19th century style was fixed. The especially large demands for peg-woodens for dolls' houses and hobbies in England may have been due to the more advanced industrial conditions there, so that

Continued on page 81.

Bisque-headed doll with kid body and bisque arms. Original homemade clothes including the bonnet. Dress is in the style of the Kate Greenaway period. Germany. c.1870s. 16in (41cm) tall.

Five fortune telling dolls. (See text.) 7in (18cm), 10in (25cm), 13in (33cm), 12in (31cm) and 18in (46cm) tall.

Clock pedlar doll (front and back views). Germany. Early 20th century. 13in (33cm) tall.

German bisque-headed doll with composition body, homemade wig, dress and underclothing. Germany. 1880s. 23in (58cm) tall. She served tea to her former owner with this tea set.

Court dolls of the Louis XVI period (1780s). Carved wood jointed bodies covered with gesso and painted. Sexed. Original costumes. 14in (36cm) tall.

OPPOSITE PAGE: Papier-mâché shoulder head doll with kid body, braided hair and all original costume including paper shoes. France. c.1840s. 19½in (50cm).

Saint Michael, a German wooden creche figure with paper wings. German. 18th century. 13in (33cm) tall.

ABOVE: Italian creche figures. Man in blue, 14in (36cm) tall. Lady, 9½in (24cm) tall. Lady in rose and blue, 9in (23cm) tall. Man in black hat, 10in (25cm) tall. Lady, 19in (48cm) tall. Probably made in Naples, Italy, a city famous for the expressive faces of their creche figures in the 18th century.

LEFT: Two Christ Child figures. The standing figure, all wood, has glass eyes. His beaded costume is later than the figure. 18th century. 21in (53cm) tall. The seated figure has a wax head, hands and feet, and cloth body. Cap has hair bangs attached. Brocade costume is later than the doll. Late 17th century. 20in (51cm) tall.

OPPOSITE PAGE: Emile Jumeau bisque-headed doll marked: "Tete Jumeau." All original, and carries a letter from the uncle of the original owner. France. c.1890. 23in (58cm) tall.

Child Jesus in ecclesiastical robes. c.1880. 18in (46cm) tall.

Papier-mâché pre-Greiner doll with kid hands, wearing homemade calico dress, painted eyes. c.1840. 20in (51cm) tall.

Continued from page 72.

there were more middle class families who could afford minor luxuries as compared with the Continent. Adults also used them for a wide range of hobbies, converting them into chessmen, pen wipers, fortune dolls or fate-ladies, pedlars or storekeepers, pincushions or dress-maker's helpers. These odds and ends of the peg-wooden story may in turn provide useful information as we learn to cross-check types of dolls against periods when certain fads were all the rage.

And so we come to the end of the second lineage of wooden dolls. Just as the peg-woodens forced the English Woodens off the market, so in turn the technological advances of the 19th century pushed the peg-woodens from an aristocratic status to the menials of the doll world. The modern automated machine, stamping plastic into dolls of all kinds, provided the final blow. Wooden dolls will have a commercial place only under the most limited conditions (say as souvenirs), though the creative "whittling urge" of the hobbyist may help them eke out a miniscule existance.

Turning back from the mechanism and results of research to its objectives, consider this phrase from Arnold's definition, previously quoted: "....it is practical as well as theoretical, trending always toward worthwhile relationships...." In the determination of these "worth-while relationships" we need all the "common sense" and any "uncommon ability" with which we might be endowed. The doll and the toy are basic tools for the education and development of the child. Whatever knowledge we as collectors derive by the research process should, in the long run, find application to that end.

Before the application of that knowledge to the child must come education of parents and other adults who have direct responsibility for the child's future. As we are dealing with the artifacts of "play," a primary agency for this form of adult education is the museum. As we have visited museums during most of the 20th century, we have watched their gradual transformation from classified oriented, with one room full of pianos, or one of American glass, or one of primitive weapons, and so on, to a functional basis in which we are offered a period living room of the French Empire, or a Victorian bedroom, or a pioneer kitchen from California. In these settings it is now possible to introduce the artifacts of childhood in their normal relationship.

Most museums of a century ago seemed to ignore the child as part of the human race. A major trend away from this concept is the recent development of children's museums, as in Indianapolis, Indiana, where the whole stress is on children's activities and the artifacts appropriate to their interests. With the more established types of museums, doll collectors, either individually or through their clubs, are finding opportunities to participate in seasonal shows, especially at Christmas, which features dolls and toys.

A few years ago the Museum of the City of New York (one of the few to maintain a continuing exhibit of dolls and toys) held a show to contrast life as we know it today with life as it was 50 years ago. Along with the artifacts of clothing, utensils, gadgets, and so forth, of adult life, there was set up, on a level convenient for a small child to see, similar artifacts of childhood.

We had an opportunity to cooperate in a satisfying adventure in museum display techniques using dolls. Philip Morrison, a teacher and puppeteer and, at the time, an art major at California State at Long Beach, was seeking a theme for his Master's thesis in display. After studying our collection he took a cue from an antique paper peep show. He designed a three section arcade so that the visitor got the impression of entering a huge peep-show. On each side of the arcade were set small windows at various heights opening into small chambers illuminated by spotlights from above. Each chamber had its own little theme based on a single doll or toy or on a grouping.

Each section was devoted to an historic period — Empire, late Victorian, and the present. Each was personified by a child — Bess, Fanny, and Joe. Bess was fictional, but Fanny and Joe were real children whose toys formed the core of the exhibits in their section. The doorway to each section was framed by a large cut-out design showing each child. Thus Bess was about nine feet tall and one had to dodge her dangling doll on entering. The cultural themes were reinforced by three continuously operating carrousel slide projectors. Each showed the children's activities as delineated in prints and books of their respective periods.

The public response to this exhibit was excellent for all age groups. In particular, the children were stimulated

Illustration 37: English School Girl, "Red Maid," from the institution of the same name in Bristol, England, which was founded about 1790. English poured wax with cloth body and wearing all original clothing. England. 9½in (24cm) tall.

by having to search out the details of each display through the small windows from various angles. It was much more exciting to them than seeing objects set up in open cases. The elements of mystery and play were there. We felt that Morrison made a real contribution to the techniques for a children's gallery.

Another area of cooperation for the doll collector is the local library. One summer, we had on loan to our city library a display of folk toys and dolls from around the world. This was used to stimulate a children's summer reading program. A perusal of the bi-monthly *Bulletin* of the Doll Collectors of America provides many examples of the various possibilities open to collectors in cooperating with local educational activities.

While intuitively recognized in diverse areas for

many years (Montessori Method, and others), modern experimental psychology and biology are demonstrating that the most important years for the intellectual development of the child is before he ever gets to school. In those years the doll and toy can play a most important part. Even the simplest crib doll may assist, not only in providing a sense of emotional security, but in stimulating the senses of touch, sight, and hearing; the coordination of form to feeling, and so on. It is in these early days that the potential genetic intellectual capacity with which the child is born is developed by the variety and richness of its environment.

It follows directly that at some point in our educational system prospective parents should be aware of this, not by a few lectures just before the wedding day, but by a continuing program such as "Family Life Education" from kindergarten (dolls' house play) through High School. These efforts are in their early stages and there is much in the details of such a course to which our special interests could make contributions, not only from the standpoint of the design of playthings, but also in the areas of publicity and public relations.

From the furtherance of these ideas it appears to us that the establishment of a "Museum of Childhood" would be most desirable. This does not mean a "Children's Museum" working with children and their activities, but a museum for adults to learn about children and the relationship of a child's environment (the artifacts of childhood) to their development from conception through adolescense. One step has been taken in this direction by the Museum of Childhood in Edinburgh, Scotland; another is the recent conversion of the Bethnel Green Collection into London's Museum of Childhood.

Such a museum can serve not only for the education of the public, but also behind the scenes as a research center. Here the collections which we have made can be studied for the significance of the plaything in the development of a culture and of the individual. The result of these studies can then be applied to improving the displays presented to the public. The increasing complexity of our modern technological culture makes it most important that every avenue contributing individual competence be exploited. In this direction we may then hope that research based on our collecting activities will lead to "worthwhile relationships."

Illustration 38: Wax-over papier-mâché doll with glass eyes. Wearing store bought dress and homemade cape and hat. c.1880. 15½in (39cm) tall. This doll is similar to Child Jesus in blue ecclesiastical robes (page 80) and possibly made by the same maker.

Illustration 39: Two wax-over papier-mâché head dolls, all original and wearing gauze store bought clothes. Wire pull eyes. Germany. Early 19th century. 13in (33cm) and 12in (31cm) tall. (These dolls came from Mrs. Schenck's attic and reportedly came to America on a Clipper Ship.)

Chapter 4

Fashion Dolls and the Fashionables

OPPOSITE PAGE: Illustration 40. Lady Abbott of Tunbridge Wells, England. Wax head, arms and legs with cloth body. Human hair inserted with hot needle. All original and costumed as she would have been presented to Queen Victoria. England. c.1880s. 26in (66cm) tall.

It is obvious that if we are researching objects from the past that have no names, and about which we know little or nothing, we will soon have to invent names before we can even discuss them. There is no harm in this, provided that we realize that such names are temporary makeshifts to be discarded as we learn more about the artifacts, and either their true names are discovered, or more suitable ones suggest themselves.

So it is with dolls. But it is most regrettable that so many of the earliest, inaccurate and misleading names for dolls have attached themselves. With official approval they have not only been retained by collectors, but are now in general use among publishers, auction houses and, disastrously, by museums.

This puts dolls in a unique and degrading position among the decorative arts, for in no other field is the nomenclature so patently amateur and absurd. We feel strongly that the antiquarian world will never take dolls seriously, until a suitable scholarly vocabulary is established.

Man has used miniature images of himself for numerous purposes in times past, many of them strange and curious. The relationship of dolls as toys for children and dolls serving these other uses is a complex and varied one, and the dividing line is often difficult to draw.

Creche and shrine figures, lay figures, funeral effigies, witchcraft images, the grave doll, the fashion doll, the kachina, the theatrical puppet and the purely decorative figurine may all, in one way or another, be closely related to the play doll. In some instances they are found to be interchangeable.

No serious doll collector goes long without studying the history of fashion, or judging the period and correctness of a particular specimen. Conversely, the availability of dolls of known history becomes of value in determining the story of fashions.

Fashion may be divided into two broad fields — the relatively stable national, provincial, or local costume, and the ever changing international styles. Style did not become of much importance until Europe began its emergence from the Dark Ages with the beginning of the Renaissance in the 14th century. At that time the growth of wealth and civilization in the great Italian City-States, such as Venice, Naples, Florence and Milan, lead to rivalry in the art of display in dress. High fashion was of

course limited to a few, the rulers and wealthy merchants. The weaving arts had developed to the point where magnificent brocades of silk, velvet and metal were available to provide flowing robes of the utmost ostentation. By the time of Columbus, Spain was beginning to develop its power and, as the controlling force over most of Europe, naturally became the leader in style. In the Court of Spain there was developed the use of the farthingale and other harnesses to hold the skirt out widely on both sides. This, together with a stiff corset for the V shaped bodice, was to set the basic silhouette for a very long time. The portraits of the Infantas by Velasquez show very good examples of this style.

"Fashion Dolls" appeared for the first time in the accounts of the French Court when the Court Embroiderer, Robert de Varennes, in the service of Charles VI, received 459 francs for a dolls' wardrobe he had made. Queen Isabeau de Baviere (1371-1435), born a Bavarian princess, sent this to her daughter, Queen Isabella of England. Before Henry IV of France's second marriage, he sent some dolls to his future bride, Marie de Medici, exp'aining, "Frotenac tells me that you wish to have some models of our fashions" (Bachmann and Hansmann).

Queen Elizabeth I of England, while successfully fending off the Spanish Armada, was conquered by their styles. In adopting them, however, she scorned their dark and drab colors, blossoming forth in brilliant hues, perhaps to distract attention from her own lack of beauty. She had a wardrobe of 3000 elaborate dresses and 800 wigs which, with characteristic vanity, she had arranged for display to the public.

By the middle of the 17th century, the center of power had swung back to France and, under the long reign of Louis XIV, that country assumed the lead in setting fashions which it has maintained fairly successfully ever since. Although not always the innovator of a new fashion, Paris was most generally the center through which it was made popular.

An anonymous lampoon of 1689 says: "And the worst is that women do not only travel to France, but have models, dressed dolls, sent which cost many thalers so that they can imitate carefully the devil's vanity."

In spite of the hostilities during the Spanish Wars of Succession (1701-1713) both countries allowed the mannequin free entry as "an act of gallentry toward the

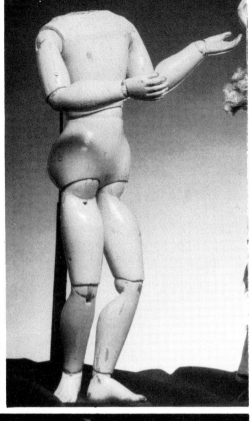

Illustration 41.
The headless
all wood body
of a Parisianne
doll showing
its articulation.
(Shown on
page 35.)

ladies." All this is related in a special report by the Abbe Prevost from the year 1704. In 1712, that is to say, while the war was still on, English papers stated: "Last Saturday, the French Doll for the year 1712 arrived at my house in King Street, Covent Garden" (Bachmann and Hansmann).

The doll had a unique relation to fashion in these early times in that it was often the mechanism by which a new fashion was put on display or sent from one country to another. This was recorded at each change of fashion and sent from Paris to London. With the difficulties of transportation in early days it was only natural that recourse would be had to smaller figures of dolls for this purpose. During the 17th and 18th centuries fashion was regarded as so important that the "grand poupe" or "fashion doll" was allowed to pass freely in times of war. Napoleon put an end to this practice.

In the colonial American newspapers it was not uncommon to see a notice like this: "To be seen at Mrs. Hannah Teat's mantua maker, at the head of Summer Street, Boston, a manikin dressed after the newest fashions of mantuas and nightgowns, and everything appertaining to women's attire, lately brought on the 'Captain White.' Ladies who choose to see it may come, or send for it. It is always ready to serve you. If you come, it will cost you two shillings, but if you send for it, seven shillings."

An essay in the *Spectator* reads: "Betty Cross-stitche's letter says she has received a French baby for the year 1712. I have taken the utmost care to have her dressed by the most famous tire-woman and mantua maker in Paris. The puppet was dressed in a cherry-colored gown and petticoat with a short working apron over it which discovered her shape to the greatest advantage."

The 18th century was known as the age of enlightenment and the middle of it marked the beginning of the Industrial Revolution. Before that time dolls and figures were made only on special order for the wealthy and the church by skilled craftsmen. They were rare. After, with the growth of the middle-classes, they were made on a production basis in wood, wax and porcelain. This made it possible for small shops and even pedlars to use dolls for the display of the newest materials.

The advances in the mechanical arts which made this possible soon produced another medium as the purveyor

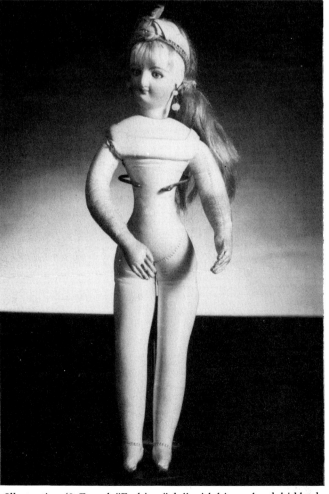

Illustration 42. French "Fashion" doll with bisque head, kid body and long braided human hair wig. France. Mid 19th century.

of fashions, the colored fashion plate. First appearing in Europe about the time of the American Revolution (1776), by the turn of the century a number of monthly ladies' magazines used them freely. Still the old custom held on a while. In 1826, a fashion doll was sent from France to Salem, Massachusetts, to Martha Derby, the dress and coiffure to be copied for her first ball. But by the early 1830s *Godey's* magazine took care of American needs.

However, the latest styles were not only on fashion dolls, they were also on the dolls made expressly for children and continued so long after the passing of the fashion doll proper. Many dolls were sold unclothed and the family talents or those of the family seamstress were devoted to providing a wardrobe. This often resulted in a costume superior to the usual shop article. For those familiar only with the dolls of the 20th century it may be difficult to realize that there were few baby or childlike dolls before the latter part of the 19th century. Only about the time of Alice in Wonderland (Illustration 38) did dolls appear that looked like children. Previously they were ladies and dressed in ladies' fashion.

These were generally not as elaborately dressed, however, as the fashion doll proper until the time of the 1870s and 1880s. At this time there was a luxury period in dolls for children; dolls with heads and limbs of fine glazed or bisque porcelain, and elaborate bodies sometimes made of wood, beautifully jointed in the manner of the classic artist's models. Such dolls had elaborate clothing, often owning a trunk with several changes of costume, corset, hand embroidered underwear and numerous accessories. These dolls are often called, we think incorrectly, "French Fashion Dolls." There is no denying they were highly fashionable but their sole object in life was to entrance fashionable little girls, or, to judge from the fashion plates, even young ladies.

Of course, any doll made as a toy or otherwise could in isolated instances be used for fashion display right up to the present day, and are at this moment being used in many show windows.

We believe the term "fashion doll" should be restricted to the period when dolls so used were the principal means of sending information on the fashions. This period ended about the time of Napoleon.

Until the last quarter of the 19th century, dolls were lady dolls, and were dressed often in fashionable ladies' clothes. However, there is a difference between the fashion doll and the doll that is merely fashionable, although the distinction is not always easy to draw. Most dolls were dressed in the fashions of their times, and, as shown in early portraits, dolls made to be played with by children were often as elegantly and elaborately dressed as the pretentious mannequins made for their elders. For instance George Washington is known to have ordered fashionably dressed dolls for his stepchild.

Now, if the distinction is difficult to make in a period in which the true fashion doll was a commercial necessity, how much more careful we should be in a period when there was no longer such a need for them. The latest date for a doll used for sending fashion is given as 1826.

An illustration from *Harpers' Magazine* of 1875 shows two little girls with a doll in a perambulator, a most fashionably dressed doll. Another illustration of 1875 shows three elaborately dressed figures marked "STYLES FOR DOLLS," not, we note, fashions for ladies. Yet another illustration, this time from 1876, shows clearly that these dolls were for children; fashionable dolls for fashionable, very young ladies.

None of the accessories which fill the trunks of the so-called fashion dolls of the third quarter of the 19th century are such as would, in our opinion, tempt "milady" to buy. They are in fact singularly unimaginative; the same enameled watch, velvet purse, feathered fan, and so forth, recurring over and over again in trunks belonging to dolls from three decades. For a fashionable lady, they would soon have become insufferably boring, but they would have delighted a child.

A most fashionable wax doll is to be seen in our illustration of Lady Abbott of Tunbridge Wells, England (Illustration 40). She wears a creme satin court dress with a long train, finished with the utmost attention to detail. The same fine stitchery has gone into the underclothes. Was she a fashion doll? No. She was bought for a small child from Hanley's European Toy Warehouse, and kept in her original box to be looked at and loved, but not played with — a best doll. These fashionable (not fashion!) dolls were toys for children.

This ultra-luxurious period for children's dolls reached its climax between 1875 and 1880. Its death knell was sounded by the ever increasing popularity of the child doll and the baby doll.

An American magazine article dated 1877 has clear indications of this change in taste: "There are fashions in dolls as in other things, and at present the little women have a fancy for infant dolls, in preference to those that represent grown Ladies." The passing mode is still well represented, as later we read: "Fine bisque dolls are from five dollars to thirty dolls, the latter are dressed in silk, with smyrna lace trimmings, in the latest style."

And still further on: "The belongings for dolls consist of everything a lady wears or uses in her house. You can buy separately every article of dolls' clothing, such as furs, corsets, fans, bustles, travelling dresses, trained dresses, cashmere shawls, Balmoral skirts of stylish, cardinal color, eyeglasses, opera glasses, lace sets, combs, brushes, powder boxes with puffs, striped stockings, and on through the list. Saratoga trunks are provided to carry them."

The article goes on to describe all sorts of other toys. Surely, the French modistes were not distributing their styles through the New York City toy shops!

Doll collecting has attracted a large and growing group of followers. It is important that they be provided with accurate information, not only for the guidance of collectors in the pursuit of their hobby, but for the sake of the general knowledge that reflects back from the systematic study in almost any hobby.

In the case of dolls, many sidelights are thrown upon social customs of past times. One of these is the authentic fashion doll. We now understand why it should not be confused with a child's toy, no matter how fashionably the latter may be dressed.

Among all the many mysteries surrounding the history of dolls, perhaps the most tantalizing is the legend of the "Fashion Dolls," the enchanting sounding mannequins used in the days before fashion magazines and fashion houses to spread the news of the latest styles. For although there is evidence enough that such figures existed, there are, to our knowledge, no known positively proven examples, only hopeful candidates and suspects.

One such candidate is in our collection. It was acquired on our 1951 trip to Europe from the National Museum in Munich, Germany, and we were assured by the curator, a most scholarly and punctilious person, that it was described in the museum's archives as a "Fashion Doll."

This from a historian with no knowledge of the contemporary American doll collectors vocabulary (Illustration 43).

The doll is a very early one and from the style of it's fashionable, regional costume dates from the first quarter of the 17th century. It is carved from wood, with arms jointed at the elbow. From the waist down, the body is simply a framework covered with linen in a tent-like manner, quite different from the cages which we find on church figures representing the Virgin. This is most interesting since it tallies with contemporary descriptions of fashion dolls, and greatly reinforces its claim.

As in so many instances, we have hints and clues as to this doll's purpose, but no proof. Mr. Nevison, the retired curator of costumes at the Victoria and Albert Museum, London, England, made a tour of the museums of Europe and America in the mid 1960s in search of authentic fashion dolls. He found, as we might have predicted, many candidates, but no absolutely proven fashion dolls.

One piece of evidence is so detailed that it seems appropriate to quote it in full. It is from the *Spectator*, the periodical published in England in 1711-1712. It is exciting to read, but it must be remembered that the *Spectator* was notoriously satyrical, and much of its material was written with tongue in cheek.

The Spectator
No. 277 Thursday, January 17, 1712

"I presume I need not inform the polite part of my readers, that before our correspondence with France was unhappily interrupted by the war, our ladies had all their fashions from thence; which the milliners took care to furnish them with by means of a jointed baby, that came regularly over once a month, habited after the manner of the most eminent toasts in Paris.

"I am credibly informed, that even in the hottest time of the war, the sex made several efforts, and raised large contributions towards the importation of the wooden mademoiselle.

"Whether the vessel they sent out was lost or taken, or whether its cargo was seized on by the officers of the custom-house as a piece of contraband goods, I have not yet been able to learn; it is however certain, that their first attempts were without success, to the no small disappointment of our whole female world; but as their constancy and application, in a matter of so great importance, can never be sufficiently commended, I am glad to find, that in spite of all opposition, they have at length carried their point, of which I received advice by the two following letters:

"Mr. Spectator, — I am so great a lover of whatever is French, that I have lately discarded an humble admirer, because he neither spoke that tongue nor drank claret. I have long bewailed in secret the calamities of my sex during the war, in all which time we have labored under the insupportable inventions of English tire-women, who, though they sometimes copy indifferently well, never can compose with that 'gout' they do in France.

"I was almost in dispair of ever more seeing a model from that dear country, when last Sunday I overheard a lady in the next pew to me whisper another, that at the Seven Stars, in King-street, Covent Garden, there was a mademoiselle completely dressed, just come from Paris.

"I was in the utmost impatience during the remaining part of the service, and as soon as it was over, having learnt the milliner's 'addresse,' I went directly to her house in King-street, but was told that the French lady was at a person of quality's in Pall Mall, and would not be back again until very late that night. I was therefore obliged to renew my visit very early this morning, and had then a full view of the dear moppet from head to foot.

"You cannot imagine, worthy sir, how ridiculously I find we have been trussed up during the war, and how infinitely the French dress excells ours.

"The mantua has no lead in the sleeves, and I hope we are not lighter than the French ladies, so as to want that kind of ballast; the petticoat has no whalebone, but sits with an air altogether gallant and degage: the coiffure is inexpressibly pretty; and, in short, the whole dress has a thousand beauties in it, which I would not have as yet made too public.

"I thought fit, however, to give you this notice, that you may not be surprised at my appearing a la mode de Paris on the next birthnight. I am, sir, your very humble servant, TERAMINTA.

"Within an hour after I had read this letter, I received another from the owner of the puppet.

"Sir, on Saturday last, being the 12th instant, there arrived at my house in King-street, Covent Garden, a French baby for the year 1712. I have taken the utmost care to have her dressed by the most celebrated tire-women and mantua makers in Paris, and do not find that I have any reason to be sorry for the expense I have been at in her clothes and importation; however, as I know no person who is so good a judge of dress as yourself, if you please to call at my house in your way to the city, and take a view of her, I promise to amend whatever you shall disapprove in your next paper, before I exhibit her as a pattern to the public. I am, sir, your most humble admirer, and most obedient servant, BETTY CROSS-STITCH.

"As I am willing to do anything in reason for the service of my country women, and had much rather prevent faults than find them, I went last night to the house of the above-mentioned Mrs. Cross-stitch. As soon as I entered, the maid of the shop, who, I suppose, was prepared for my coming, without asking me any questions, introduced me to the little damsel, and ran away to call her mistress.

"The puppet was dressed in a cherry-coloured gown and petticoat, with a short working apron over it, which discovered her shape to the most advantage. Her hair was cut and divided very prettily, with several ribands stuck up and down in it. The milliner assured me, that her complexion was such as was worn by all the ladies of the best fashion in Paris. Her head was extremely high, on which subject having long since declared my sentiments, I shall say nothing more to it at the present. I was also offended at a small patch she wore on her breast, which I cannot suppose is placed there with any good design.

"Her necklace was of an immoderate length, being tied before in such a manner, that the two ends hung down to her girdle; but whether these supply the place of kissing-strings in our enemy's country, and whether our British ladies have any occasion for them, I shall leave to their serious consideration.

"After having observed the particulars of her dress, as I was taking a view of it altogether, the shop-maid, who is a pert wench, told me the Mademoiselle had something very curious in the tying of her garters; but as I pay due respect even to a pair of sticks when they are under petticoats, I did not examine into that particular. Upon the whole, I was well enough pleased with the appearance of this gay lady, and the more so because she was not talkative, a quality very rarely to be met with in the rest of her country women.

"As I was taking my leave, the milliner farther informed me, that with the assistance of a watch-maker, and the ingenious Mr. Powel, she had also contrived another puppet, which by the help of several little springs to be wound up within it, could move all its limbs, and that she had sent it over to her correspondent in Paris to be taught the various leanings and bending of the head, the risings of the bosom, the courtesy and recovery, the genteel trip, and the agreeable jet, as they are now practised at the court of France.

"She added that she hoped she might depend upon having my encouragement as soon as it arrived; but as this was a petition of too great importance to be answered extempore, I left her without a reply, and made the best of my way to Will Honeycomb's lodgings, without whose advice I never communicate anything to the public of this nature." (This essay is attributed to Budgell.)

Gibson Girl

At a time when the United States was first feeling its strength as a world power, young Charles Dana Gibson gave to his public a feminine image; an image strangely aristocratic and polished for a country which had long made a fetish of its pioneer and homespun origins. This was the Gibson Girl — tall, slender, refined, aristocratic, with finely chiselled delicate features and yet friendly, warm and vigorous.

The unsuitability of the child's toy doll for use as a "messenger of fashion" is now being well recognized as most writers are making references to the "so-called French Fashion Dolls" and the "so-called Milliner's Models." In addition to the unsuitability of the doll's jointing systems, the lack of individuality in toy dolls' faces would not appeal to display designers wishing to put a real flair into their exhibits.

For this reason "dressmaker's dolls" or "fashion mannequins" in the limited use to which they were used after the fashion plate came in were very often individually modelled, especially in the sizes corresponding to toy dolls. For this purpose wax was well suited and a group for the gay nineties is shown in the Schott Collection in the Fine Arts Museum in Santa Barbara, California, and another group used by Wanamaker is in the Chester County Historical Museum, West Chester, Pennsylvania.

Illustration 43. Munich Fashion Doll. Wooden head and arms; no legs. Wearing original costume, lined with net for preservation. A true fashion doll, according to the International Museum in Munich, Germany, where she was purchased. Germany. 1615-1625. 23in (58cm) tall.

It has been reported that seasonal displays of such individually designed mannequins drew the country dressmakers to the big city to bring their art up to date. Our photograph shows a less usual form of a display figure for the Gibson period, with fabric face and kid arms modelled over a wire frame. The craftsman has developed to the full those features of the style which, while concealing all, even to the white kid high shoes, emphasized the feminine shape in all its glory. This figure was presented to the Escondido Historical Society, Escondido, California, on the occasion of the city's 75th anniversary by the Mathes (Illustration 44).

We feel strongly that it is never too late to correct our mistakes, in this instance, as in many others. Here we have presented the evidence. It is very simple to distinguish between the fashion and the fashionable doll. The constant review and refinement of knowledge in other fields — silver, ceramics, furniture — is a hallmark of professionalism. It is high time that this professionalism entered our beloved world of dolls.

U.F.D.C. Glossary

In 1978 the United Federation of Doll Clubs, Inc. published its *Glossary* to improve communications and standardize terms. This booklet should be in every collectors library. On the study committee to establish a common vocabulary were Larry L. Belles, Dorothy S. Coleman, Elizabeth Ann Coleman, Sarah Kocher, Z. Frances Walker and Margaret Whitton. The United Federation of Doll Clubs and *Doll Reader* subscribers were invited to participate. The dolls used came from the Margaret Strong Museum.

The time is ripe for re-evaluating the *Glossary* and for establishing names in areas that are misunderstood. Many new books are being published without reference to the *Glossary*.

At the end of our chapter on fashion dolls seems to be an appropriate place to make some suggestions:

Fashion Dolls — conveyors of fashion before the fashion plate (late 18th century).

Fashionable Doll — any doll that is stylishly dressed.

Milliner's Models — coiffeured papier-mâché.

Dutch Doll — Not to be confused with German peg-woodens.

English Wooden — use instead of Queen Anne or Maryannegeorgian.

Doll — a new definition is needed here.

Illustration 44. Gibson Girl with parasol. Cloth face, wrapped wire body, and kid arms and legs. Real hair wig. Original clothing. 14in (36cm) tall. (Donated to the Escondido [California] Historical Society by the authors.)

Chapter 5

Fortune Teller Dolls

From time to time, adults intrude upon the child's jurisdiction and appropriate his toys to their own amusement. In particular the doll has been so used in many ways — such as, a quilting party scene, as pedlars or shopkeepers, as chess pieces, and among these are the fortune teller dolls.

The more usual form of such a doll or adult plaything is to provide the doll with a skirt or underskirt made up of many pieces of folded paper sewn to a cloth underskirt or assembled on a tape which is then tied around the waist of the doll. We have a pair of these dolls from England, one with fortunes for men and the other for women. These are placed on the crude Tyrolean peg-woodens of the mid to late 19th century. They are 13in (33cm) tall. The paper pieces are of many bright colors: red, green, pink, lavender, yellow, blue, on the outside and white on the inside when unfolded.

Sample fortunes for men are:

Your lot, dear sir, is doubly blest,
two wives you'll have, of wives the best.

Come pop the question, Sir, don't tarry,
I'm sure you're old enough to marry.

Your love so long has had her way,
Try to rule she probably may.

A black eyed girl attracts your eye,
Ask her, she'll not your suit deny.

You'll marry a poor silly girl under twenty
Who, ere you are fifty, your coffers will empty.

Sample fortunes for women:

Grieve not lady, though tis late
You shall have a wealthy mate.

Single you are and will remain,
This news, I am sure, will give you pain.

Not married yet! The men are blind.
The loss is theirs, never mind.

A clergyman, both good and kind;
Your hand and heart with his will bind.

The Fates, hardhearted Fates, decree
A staid old maid thou wilt be.

There is one common characteristic to these English fortunes; they are concerned in a thoroughly Victorian sentimental way with affairs of romance and marriage. Our second example from England operates in a different way. Her cone shaped hat identifies her as a witch. She

has a long white cane in one hand and can be twirled on a pivot. When she comes to rest, the cane will point at one of a number of fortunes spread around her feet. No fortunes came with her so we presume they were lost. She is 8½in (22cm) tall overall. While she wears the red cape typical of the late 19th century, she is a peg-wooden of the early 19th century.

The color illustration on page 74 was once in the D'Allemagne collection, and is French. She is 12in (31cm) tall, has a papier-mache head with a wig and an all kid body. The painted eyes are of the peculiar greenish blue used in the early half of the 19th century. The many fortunes are written in French; mostly short verses. On the front and back of her black paper tunic are astrological symbols in silver paper. On the chest is a comet. On one sleeve is the man in the moon and on the other is Saturn with its rings. On her back is the sun with rays and a star.

Sample fortunes are:

I know him
Lots of heart but little sense.

Love banishes fear.

Everybody loves you,
Take care of your own heart.

Unfaithful.

Cupid already meditates revenge
For your disdain.

Beware of Judas' kiss.

The future has in store more
beautiful days for you.

There is no glory for those
who strive for it too intensely.

Oh! Be fearful to learn of your unhappy fate.

If want to have people say good things of you
then do not brag about yourself.

The general tone of these fortunes is didactic, warning of evils and suggesting the good. More interesting fortunes are to be found on the Tyrolean peg-wooden doll shown in the color illustration on page /4. This doll is 20in (51cm) tall and is the same as the one shown in Illustration 120 on page 129 of *Dolls and Puppets* by Max von Boehn. It still has the ball and socket joints characteristic of the late 18th century and the first part of the 19th century.

The upper garment is of velvet, a fawn color faded

from apricot. The skirt is made of various colored stripes of satin, velvet and brocade. On her chest is a small broach of white rays with two metallic insignia, the lower being simply decorative but the upper having the form of a running dog. The fortunes, over 100 in number, are written on the reverse side of heart-shaped pieces of wallpaper. This wallpaper was dated for us by the Decorative Arts Department of the Victoria and Albert Museum as being of the 1770s.

All of these fortunes were written in verse in a slightly archaic French. We have literal translations of all and have put some of them into English rhyme. Two of them refer explicitly to their fortune telling function:

> *Today, they wear triumphant airs,*
> *Tomorrow, ruin to their affairs.*
> *They will suffer deep disgrace*
> *While you again will raise your face.*

Among these many fortunes, there is at least one which proved to be correct:

> *Forget not my pronouncement of your doom*
> *When one day you leave this land of France.*
> *Some strange land will give you room,*
> *Your sighs we hear; but of return, no chance.*

That land turned out to be the United States of America. The internal evidence of these verses indicates that the author of them was actuated to protest against the dissolute and irresponsible activities of Versailles' decadence before the French Revolution, the same court that produced the sexually explicit figures commonly referred to as "Court Dolls." We have no documentary evidence that this is the history of these fortunes, but a considerable number of those fleeing the Revolution settled in Pennsylvania, not too far from where the fortunes were found near Princeton, New Jersey. They could well have been brought over at that time and then tied to a later figure in this country.

The examples which we have discussed so far, appear to be the one-of-a-kind or home-hobby type. The fortune teller shown in the color illustration on page 74 is, however, definitely a commercially made product. The fortunes are printed, and on several of the leaves is this statement: "Patents Pending in the U.S. and Abroad. The Sibyl Fortune Telling Doll Co., 1310 S. Hobart Ave., Los Angeles, Calif." There is a booklet of instructions as to how to use this fortune teller which unfortunately we do not have. At the bottom of each page is printed the name of an ancient god, such as Mercury, Juno, Cupid, Apollo and so forth.

Pink leaves, for example, are labelled Apollo and have answers to ten questions numbered 41 through 50. However, the answer to question 41 on one Apollo sheet is: *No, sleep on the matter.* On another Apollo sheet the answer to 41 is: *Plan it, then do it without hesitating.* On a third, the answer is: *Don't do it if you are uncertain.* On another: *Yes, now or never.* And on another: *Do it quickly and resolutely.*

Thus the Sibyl is prepared to provide quite different answers to the same question depending on which pink leaf is selected.

The figures general appearance suggests a gypsy. The symbolic figures on her coat are those which we usually associate with witchcraft — a row of cats around the bottom, a witch flying on a broom, a bat, a wishbone, a new moon, a cat, a horseshoe and a snake. The kind of questions and answers provided by this rather modern example reflect a comfortable workaday world, a number of them relating to matters of romance but more to business affairs and the ordinary doings of a settled society.

It is often observed that children's toys reflect the adult world. Here the adults reveal more of themselves, their times and their foibles through their appropriation of the child's toy to their own ends.

Chapter 6

Dolls' Houses and Doll's House Dolls

RIGHT and OPPOSITE PAGE: Illustrations 45A, 45B and 45C: English dolls' house furnishings and dolls dating from the 18th century to the middle of the 19th century.

We have earlier on discussed dolls' houses intended for children. We had been collecting for some years before we realized that before the high Victorian era achieved momentum, dolls' houses were as much — and indeed more — a pleasure for adults, than as toys for children.

The revelation came to us when we acquired from England a late 18th century dolls' house. It was our most exciting adventure in collecting. In 1954 we responded to a small advertisement in *Hobbies* magazine placed by a Mr. A. Solman, then an antiques dealer in London, England. We first obtained from him several very fine individual items, such as the plume doll, a wax face pedlar, a dolls' house size rag doll of 1730, and a pair of peg-woodens. These were costumed and with large hats, quite similar to the Countess of Jedburgh and the Duchess of Orleans as illustrated in *Queen Victoria's Dolls*, by Frances H. Low. The pedlar was a peg-wooden doll whose wax face was really just a mask, paper-thin.

But the last acquisition was the best: a group of 20 dolls' house dolls, about half in very good condition, and well over 100 pieces of furniture, fireplace fittings, dishes, books, utensils, and knick-knacks. Mr. Solman had meticulously listed and priced every item separately, down to the last little wine glass, and then quoted an overall price. After a little struggle with our budget we took the lot, and with no regrets.

Mr. Solman had purchased the lot as a unit from an elderly man who recalled playing with them as a child before they were relegated to the attic. Most of the pieces are Georgian in style with some early Victorian. Accordingly, it was probably assembled and played with by two or three generations. The two oldest dolls were made with heads and hands of kid. They were most likely the grandparents of the doll family. He is in knee breeches, his clothes beautifully tailored and with fine details like his neckcloth and watch fob of seals. She is in informal morning dress. They are so skillfully done as to suggest a professional maker. A family of kid faced dolls' house dolls of the early Regency (1810-1820) period is to be seen at the Doll Museum in Warwick, England, and of course there are also the kid faced pedlar dolls, commercially made in England, which bear a striking resemblance to the pair here.

The fourposter bed is splendidly carved and has silk brocade hangings and coverlet. The brass warming pan with its wooden handle was filled with coals and thrust between the icy linen sheets on cold nights. The dressing table, with a glazed cotton skirt and cover that matches the bed, has a tilting mirror and many toilet articles: hair brush and comb, jewelry rack, jars of ointments, besides a candlestick. Here, the rarest item is the pair of steel curling irons.

The bedroom fireplace is ornamented with brass candlesticks and a rare blue Bristol glass jug. The washstand, a handsome piece with ivory drawer pulls, stands near by furnished with its jug, bowl and chamber pot, and an ivory toothbrush. In the warmest place, before the fire, the painted tin hip bath is placed with its matching can to transport water, and painted tin slop pail. Towels warm on the mahogany towel horse, and so do handmade slippers. A handsome, full length cheval mirror is a valuable aid to dressing. The chair is an early carved and painted wooden one, with a simulated rush seat.

On the bureau's marble top stand a second pair of brass candlesticks, early and turned, beside an unusual Bristol glass bird, a hand held fire screen, a clothes brush, and a marvelous penknife with a safety guard and a tortoise shell handle.

This was a musical family, for in the drawing room we find papa and one of his daughters with their guitars and their music stand. Mama and the rest of the family listen attentively. They are all early peg-wooden dolls from the Grödner Tal, and two of the male dolls are of special interest. Evidently the children did not like the feminine hairstyle of the peg-wooden dolls for their men, so they cut off their heads and replaced them with papier-mache heads more to their liking. These appear to be an early type, as the eye colors are deeper and more brilliant than those of any other we have seen. Then, due to a change in hairstyling, they sewed on wigs of silk floss.

The drawing room contains beautiful furniture — a chest with simulated marble top and ivory supports; a table with drop leaves; and a second pedestal table with drop leaves and drawer. The desk, with its hinged ledge, has drawers and cubbyholes for papers, both standing and hanging letter racks, and a most unusual adjustable leather-seated stool. There is also a beautiful lap desk with brass inlays.

The tea equipage includes a lead lined tea caddy with brass feet, japanned tea trays, and a splendid porcelain tea

Illustrations 46A and 46B: English rag dolls' house doll with embroidered face and quill arms (front and back views). c.1730. 4in (10cm) tall.

service for six, with wide bands of gold.

The long-case clock did not come from the attic, but it matches the style of the other furniture. Bob's father's watch fits well in the case. There is much fine glassware, including a pair of blue Bristol vases which may be hyacinth glasses. There are four prints, varnished to look like oil paintings, and their gold paper frames are decorated with embossed motifs to imitate carved and gilded wood. A handsome six-light glass chandelier illuminates this room.

The dining room furniture is equally handsome. There are four very fine sabre-leg chairs (two of them in the drawing room) with red leather seats and inlaid back rests. The miniature makers of that day were exquisite craftsmen. The sideboard has cupboards, one of which holds a wine store, and their doors have raised panels. The knife boxes contain both knives and matching Georgian two-prong forks.

The wine cooler is wicker with a zinc lining and five dark green "glass" bottles, archaic in shape, and made surprisingly of wood. Here is a dinner service with painted garlands and more fine early glass, including an unusual engraved bumper. A Grödner Tal butler is in attendance.

The kitchen is always the most fascinating room in any dolls' house, and here we find a very early kitchen range. The fire is still in an open grate on the front of the stove, but on one side of this grate we have a warming oven, and on the other side a water tank with a faucet for hot water. Just in front of the grate is a metal rack standing on the floor with a large flat pan at the bottom. Suspended from the rack is a short chain with a hook from which the meat was hung to roast. Inside the cylinder was a clockwork which kept the meat rotating

slowly before the open fire. This device was called a "bottle jack." The drippings were caught in the large pan below. Thus there was a reason for the term "dripping," which we still use, although in the modern oven they no longer drip.

On the lowest shelf of the fireplace we notice a long horizontal cylinder, the candle box. Candles were commonly made at that time from mutton tallow (very tempting to mice), so candle boxes were made of metal and often hung on the wall, out of the small rodents reach. Among the candlesticks kept in the kitchen is a particularily interesting one. The candle is mounted on a cylindrical box which contains the flint, steel and tinder for lighting the first fire in the morning. There are many kitchen accessories — a lantern hanging on the wall, coal scuttle, pots and pans of all sizes, a funnel, a grater, a colander, a handsome copper coffeepot on an unusually tall brass trivet, and an equally handsome copper kettle.

There is a schoolroom or nursery, full of Grödner Tal children with their governesses and tutor. There are enchanting toys, an ivory bilboquet and an ivory top, and several tiny peg-wooden dolls. There is a wonderful early scrapbook full of engravings of gentlemen seats, a drawing book full of accomplished water colors less than an inch square, and three handwritten stories, the latest dated 1843.

Children's toys mirror the adult world, and this is especially evident in the fitting of a dolls' house. This one is most interesting reflecting as it does not only one or two generations of the same family but, in its seriousness, adult interest and pleasure. There is much here to tell us of past customs and how home life was developing, both at the end of the 18th century and at the beginning of Queen Victoria's long reign.

Chapter 7

The French "Court Dolls" Puzzle — Jealousy Dolls and Dummy Boards

As doll collecting grows more and more popular, and bigger doll books with larger and more beautiful illustrations proliferate, it is easy, especially for new collectors, to disdain the early books with their black and white illustrations often poorly printed, and their widely inaccurate findings — the results of well-meaning but amateurish research.

This is a short-sighted attitude, for in those old books many dolls are recorded that have long since vanished, and among the conjectures facts are recorded that would otherwise be lost.

Janet Johl's book *The Fascinating Story of Dolls* was first published in 1941. On page 46 is shown a group of seven wooden dolls ascribed to the court of Marie Antoinette and Louis XVI. On page 44 of the text it states: "Mrs. Isole Dorgan reported a remarkable group of very rare historical French dolls of carved wood, originally owned by the Princesse Lamballe, and played with by Marie Antoinette and adults of the gay French Court in 1776. These dolls represent men and women of the court and are not toys for children. Mrs. Dorgan writes: 'they are Marie Antoinette, Louis XVI, Princesse Lamballe, a gentleman of the court, the tallest man of the royal family, not identified, Duc de Provence, Louis XVIII, with double curls, and Duc d'Artois, with one curl, Louis X, Duc de Barton, and Chevalier d'Eon. At the Exposition des Costumes Anciens, held in Paris at the Musee des Arts Decoratifs, in October 1909, beautiful examples of Louis XVI dolls, well preserved, were shown. Eight ladies and seven gentlemen in complete costumes of elaborate brocades and laces, with high heeled shoes, high coiffures and tiny jewels, were displayed.' The dolls seemed to have been very like the ones which Mrs. Dorgan now has, and may even be the same."

Although Mrs. Dorgan states that her dolls represent specific individuals the photograph shows three female and four male figures, but she has only two female names and seven male names, plus one unidentified. Without further documentation we would therefore doubt these ascriptions. Also, while the carving is fairly elaborate it is not such as to give the feeling of portraiture.

In the early 1960s, we acquired a male and female figure very like these (see color photo on page 76). Our female figure has facial characteristics practically identical with those of the right hand figure in the book, but with

four side curls instead of two. The dress and hat styles are also very similar. There was also a similar doll in the late Madame de Galéa's collection in which the styles and hair carving technique are almost identical, but with the four side curls parallel and horizontal.

The specific adult purpose for these toys is puzzling to us. If Mrs. Johl were writing now, she would surely use the word "licentious" instead of "gay," in the phrase above. Elsewhere Janet Johl refers to "dolls representing ladies of the demimonde, during the days of court corruption preceding the Revolution, dolls such as fashionable gentlemen might consider appropriate gifts for their mistresses." This most probably refers to the Dorgan figures.

There are, however, several more interesting points to be considered. On both our figures the genitals are carved in detail and painted. In addition, the jointing systems on our figures suggest that they were puppets. The man has no joints at the knees but at the hips, elbows and shoulders the joints are made of two interlaced wire loops, providing a very free joint. While the lady has mortice and tenon joints at the hips, these are very loose and free. At the knees, elbows and shoulders she also has the loose loop joints. These interlaced loop joints were also used on 18th century marionettes and, interestingly, such marionettes had the features carved overly large and strong, so as to carry well visually to an audience. Most of these "Court Dolls" have similarly carved features.

There is another consideration that may throw some light on their status. Mrs. Dorgan's dolls are said to have belonged to the Princesse Lamballe. For some years before the Revolution she was Marie Antionette's closest friend and confidante. She was appointed superintendant of the Queen's household. This meant that she had much to do with the arrangement of entertainments, theatricals and other amusements, all to please a group of the most disolute and dissipated young aristocrats. The populace came to regard the Princesse Lamballe as responsible for the most unsavory intrigues at the court. When she was executed during the Revolution, the mob took vengence on her in a most sadistic manner — she was literally torn to pieces.

While there is no trace of the strings needed to operate marionettes, it seems plausible that because of the orgiastic parties enjoyed by this liscentious court, our

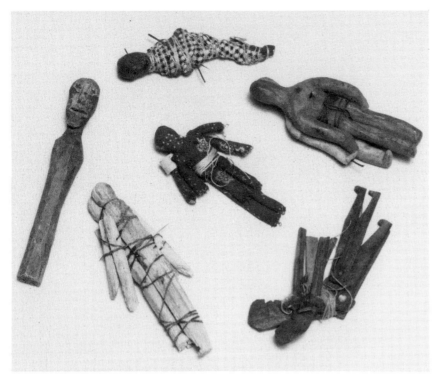

Illustration 47: Jealousy dolls from Mexico. Late 19th century. 3 to 5in (8 to 13cm) tall.

RIGHT: Illustration 48: Presence in the house (dummy board) figure painted on wood panel and representing a young girl. England. c.1675-1705.

figures may have been carried and animated by hand in pornographic byplay. In the 18th century, pantins were very popular as adult entertainment, and there are references to pantins with similar bawdy functions.

Over the years a number of other examples of these dolls have come to light, and more and more their fantastic nature becomes evident. Their sharp, unkindly little faces seem more and more like caricature, and this re-enforces the theory that they are portraits. Their genital structures are often abnormal and bizarre — perhaps crude jokes against rivals or lovers?

A few of these dolls are in original 18th century costume, but many have been redressed. An alarming number are unmistakably of recent origin, late 19th or early 20th century, compounding our mystery. Was there perhaps a second cycle of licentious parties, in the "naughty" 1890s, or the degenerate 1920s?

This is all conjecture, but at least it offers a feasible explanation for these extraordinary toys.

Two other kinds of adult dolls in our collection should be mentioned briefly. One is a series of jealousy dolls found in Mexico in the late 19th century by an archeologist from Chicago, Illinois. These figures are in pairs, tied together and run through by pins or nails. They are made from different materials such as cloth, wood, and a kind of clay. One can only imagine the voodoo rites that might have accompanied the making and pairing of these dolls, perhaps by a jealous husband or boyfriend. They are very primitive (Illustration 47).

The second unique figure is called a dummy board (presence in the house), a trompe l'oeil 17th century figure about 41in (104cm) tall, painted on a slab of wood and cut out like a huge paper doll. These figures seemed to serve in a variety of ways. They might stand by a fireplace and keep a lonely old lady company. In a grand house, they could people a small stage that could be a part of such an establishment. Or, as in our case, she hangs on the wall as a beautiful piece of decorative art. Her origin is English and the costume and high hairdo dates her in the latter part of the 17th century (Illustration 48).

Chapter 8

Cased Dolls

Illustration 50: A memorial wax-over papier-mâché case doll. Germany. c.1840. Doll is 13in (33cm) tall; case is 14in (36cm) tall.

In the course of collecting, we have naturally found many examples which have been diverted from their original purpose. When dolls or related figures have been sealed in cases, they are not available to the child as a plaything. There are five such examples in our collection where encasing has occurred for a variety of reasons.

The first and earliest case came from the gravestone of a child in New England. Mrs. Imogene Anderson acquired it from a member of the family. The reason for this example is an emotional one — to memorialize a deceased child. The case is a sturdy one, carved from a single block of wood. When the glass front was puttied in place, it was completely weatherproof (Illustration 49).

The doll is an English wooden with a plaster face. It is one of the last of the line of such dolls. We think that perhaps the wig was made from a lock of the dead child's hair. The case is 10¾in (27cm) long, and 4½in (12cm) wide. *The Album of American History, Colonial Period,* by James Truslow Adams, has a picture of this doll on page 336.

Our second example of a cased doll was sold to us as a gravestone doll. We feel this designation to be incorrect, as the case is assembled from several pieces of wood and is glued together. Obviously it would have come apart in the weather, even though the glass front is puttied in place (Illustration 50).

There are two blonde locks of hair by the head and three of darker tones by the feet, indicating the deaths of more than one child who had played with it. This memorial probably hung in a bedroom or parlour and is a grim reminder of the high rate of child mortality of those times.

This doll is wax-over papier-mâché, with blonde hair set in a cleft in the top of the head. The glass eyes are blue with black pupils. The body appears to be cloth with kid forearms and shoes. The necklace is an elaborate series of tiny multi-colored strings of beads. The case is 14in (36cm) long and 6¾in (17cm) wide.

There are no indications that our third example was a memorial doll (Illustration 51). It may have been encased simply to preserve it as an heirloom. Another possibility is that it may have been considered too fragile or expensive for children to handle. The doll has a cast wax head which has a lightly painted indication of hair. The tiny eyes are of black glass. The forearms and hands are of cast wax. The dress is in the high waisted, classical style which was used for children before adults. The doll is surrounded by dried flowers. A label pasted on the back of the case reads: "THIS WAX DOLL WAS GIVEN IN 1779 TO MRS. DUNN OF SOUTH CERNEY IN GLOOUSTERSHIRE, ENGLAND. THE GREAT GRANDMOTHER OF MRS. KATE BAKER, NEWPORT OWNER OF THE DOLL." The case is 13½in (34cm) tall and 5½in (14cm) wide.

Our fourth cased doll is a wax-over papier-mâché with wire-pull sleeping eyes. It has a cloth body and blue kid forearms. It is dressed in a white satin shroud and bonnet. The case is shaped like a coffin and is very heavy. The inner and outer coating is cement painted black. The length is 14in (36cm) (Illustration 52). We were puzzled as to why the case was shaped like a coffin. Then we read an article in a folklore magazine about a custom once practiced in an area around the North Sea. When a sailor was lost at sea, a surrogate figure was substituted for the body at the funeral service. Could possibly this doll in a coffin have been used in such a ceremony for a lost child?

Our last example (Illustration 53) is very different from the first four. With such a colorful and festive air, perhaps she was designed to be carried in a procession on a saint's day. This wax doll has a garland of paper flowers around the short white wooly hair on her head, and more such flowers line the top back of the case. The background is a brown and white patterned wallpaper which sparkles with a gold fleck or glitter (Illustration 53). The doll is tightly wrapped and dressed in layers of white net edged with more gold glitter. There is no indication that she had arms nor, indeed, much of a body. The same gold on her frilly wrappings is used to outline a design on her chest, including a cross, hence the religious connection. This case is 13in (33cm) long, 8in (20cm) high and 3¼in (8cm) deep. The glass front, top and sides are held together with bright blue and brown passe-partout.

The word "GERMANY" is to be seen among the wrappings, and here is another clue. Commercially made, such little shrines were — and still are — popular gifts for children on saints' days and Christmas, in Catholic countries. Perhaps this doll, like many others, represents the baby Jesus.

The placing of dolls in cases is, of course, quite at odds with their original purpose — to be a toy for a child to

Illustration 51: Wax heirloom case doll. Germany. 1779. 10in (36cm) tall.

play with and love. Their appearance in this form represents some special circumstance or event. This could be a desire to preserve an heirloom, make a decorative room display, memorialize a child, or to use for educational or ceremonial purposes.

Illustration 52: Coffin doll. Wax-over papier-mâché head, dressed in white satin shroud and wearing pink kid gloves. Wire-pull eyes. Coffin made of heavy concrete. Germany. Early 19th century. 12in (31cm) tall.

BELOW: Illustration 53: Festival case doll with wax head. Germany. 19th century. 10½in (27cm) tall.

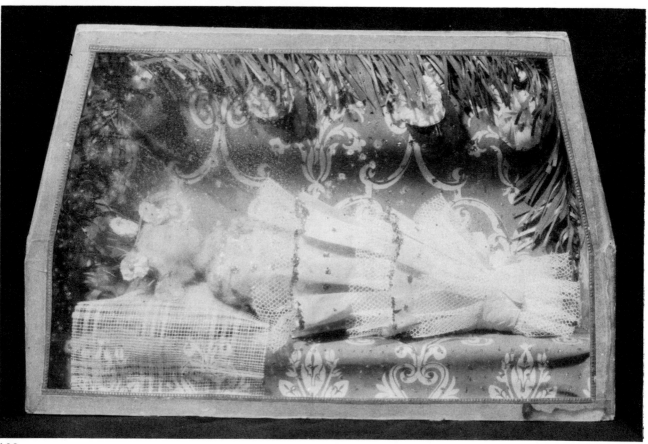

Chapter 9

The Emergence of Childhood

The history of childhood through the ages has been a sad and disturbing story. High mortality, indifference and brutality had been their lot until fairly recent times. Child labor, and apprenticing children as young as seven or eight into the mines and other menial jobs, was the norm. Young aristocrats faired no better. From a tender age they were treated as young adults, and subjected to a rigorous education. This included Greek and Latin, French and German, philosophy and architecture.

For boys there was also deportment, fencing and riding (the "haute ecole"), not to mention the management of an estate and its menials. For girls, there were the ladylike accomplishments, including fine needlework, drawing and painting, the arts of singing, dancing and conversation, poetic composition, and performance on harp and harpsichord.

No allowance was made for their immaturity; standards were rigid and punishment harsh. These children often grew up away from their parents, with governesses and tutors, in conditions less comfortable than those of their servants.

The concept that from birth the child is a growing, learning individual who reaches successful maturity through the exposure to a rich, kindly environment, started in the 16th century. In that century, Michel Montaigne (France, 1533-1594) observed that play is the child's work, and we have added "toys are his tools."

Following Montaigne, a series of other great scholars emerged who were troubled by the child's unfortunate condition. Some others who made the largest contribution after Montaigne are: John Locke (England, 1632-1704), Johann Pestalizzi (Switzerland 1746-1827), Fredrick Froebel (Germany, 1782-1852), John Dewey (America, 1859-1946) and Maria Montessori (Italy, 1870-1952). Each person on this list came from a different country, yet each had a similar goal. This gives us a common background to draw upon when we study the beginnings of child culture as we know it today.

Not until the 18th century did society begin to develop a loving approach to children. This was considered the age of enlightenment and there was a growing belief that nature was inherently good. In 1643, John Locke published *Thoughts Concerning Education*; it was reprinted nineteen times before 1761. His hopes were to arouse interest in the child, and he disapproved of flogging children to make them learn. Books that parents approved of were directed towards children. By 1744, John Newbery published *The Little Pocket-Book* which captured the imagination of both children and their parents. The Newbery family published well into the 19th century. Our best resource for early children's books is called *Early Childrens' Books*, published by the Pierpont Morgan Library in New York City.

A delightful book published by the Bucks County Historical Society in 1958, gives us a series of journals kept by the students of the Andrews School from 1837-1842. It is transcribed and beautifully illustrated by Ellen Swartzlander. This was an elementary school for boys, and the course of study included Latin, Greek, mathematics, English, rhetoric and geography. As this was a boarding school, every moment of the day and evening was planned ahead. Teachers kept a record of student merits in their books which covered class work, attendance, deportment, care of books, neatness and diligence. There were also Sunday rules and regulations. Walks into the rural sections of the community were permitted, but downtown was off limits. Students were allowed only to associate with each other.

Every effort was made to develop a sense of responsibility in the boys. Students shared in the teaching and managed the field trips. If the rules of the school were disobeyed, severe punishment could result, including whipping. The harshest punishment was to send the boy home. Student elections were held, and weekly reports submitted by student committees. Much emphasis was placed on spelling and reading aloud. Discipline problems were handled by Reverend Andrews, usually a stick applied to the backside and a trip to bed in the attic where it was very cold. Tale telling was considered a serious offense.

The students shared in community experiences also. They prepared for a July 4th celebration, and marched in the city parade. When Siamese twins were on view at the Temperance House, the boys were allowed to see them. Some students sang in the church choir, and the student body supported their concerts. A motion was made to thank Mr. Mecaskey, a guest astronomer, and Mr. Kuhn, a portrait painter. So much for cultural enrichment.

Reverend Andrews was hard on boys who had not learned their catechism, keeping them inside until it was

Illustration 54: Jubilee Dancers. Black carved wood figures wearing all original costumes. An American patented mechanical toy. Late 19th century.

Illustration 55: Two musician pull toys. German bisque dolls. All original. c.1890. 9in (23cm) tall.

memorized. If some unfortunate student talked during prayers at breakfast, a ruler was applied to his hand. In this mid 19th century, discipline was still harsh, and scholarly expectations very high. It was still not an easy time for children to grow up in. The emerging child still suffered in the adult world.

In this collecting business, we have gradually raised the questions: What is the value in it? What can we learn from it? How and to whom are toys important?

There are many to whom greater knowledge of toys (of which the doll is a specific type) will be of interest and value. To the parent, the toy is not merely to keep the child occupied but to aid in his emotional and mental growth. To the teacher, the toy can facilitate instruction. To the psychologist, it may be a tool for evaluating behavior and development. To the archeologist, the anthropologist and the historian, the toy is an "artifact" reflecting facets of the culture and technology of its time. To the economist, it may be a factor in manufacture and trade. To the philosopher, it may symbolize the spirit of an age. To the artist, it may offer a medium for communication and a subject for his artistic expression. To the collector, it may provide an aesthetic pleasure, a cultural growth, a therapy or an investment.

To the child, the toy is something to "play" with, to have fun with, to explore, to excite a world of fantasy, to satisfy his curiosity and to observe the relations between cause and effect. Again this is summed up in Montaigne's statement: "Play is the child's work." The doll has a special place, not only for girls, but also for boys, in the understanding of family and human relationships. For it is made not only to represent an infant or small child, but all the members of the family and of society in general.

Of all these interests it is that relating to the child which appears to us to be of the greatest importance. What toys and in what way do they contribute to the development of the child? Clues as to what toys come directly from the artifacts of the past, those which we find persisting through the ages, such as the rattle, the hoop, the top, the pull toy, the doll and miniatures of a wide range of adult artifacts.

We know that half of what one learns by age 17 has been learned by age five. When asked in what years man learned the most, Darwin is reported to have said "the first three." Another viewpoint puts it this way: "What is

done to develop a child's brain by age four, determines how much he is capable of learning by the time he is old enough to vote. Experience is showing that costly attempts at compensatory education have been relatively ineffective in improving a high school drop-out's capacity to learn. If these statements are even approximately true, it means that our democratic school system, using half of the average communities local taxes, is being seriously handicapped. Recent research shows that parents can assure a higher mental capacity in their children before they enter school.

We are not born with a fixed brain into which it is only necessary to pour knowledge. We are born with an inherited potential for mental ability, but the degree to which this ability is developed depends on our environment, principally during the pre-school years. The physical brain grows most rapidly during the first four years, reaching 90% of its final weight in that period. If, during that growth period, the environment does not properly foster the brain's growth and development, the child will be permanently handicapped.

These are broad statements, but the evidence being piled up by psychological studies and animal experimentation point strongly to their credibility. The important conclusion is this: Parents have in their hands, in the pre-school years, the power to largely determine the future capability and success of their children. They have two major ways of accomplishing this. They first must safeguard their inherited potential with proper prenatal care, and with proper nutrition in the pre-school years. Secondly, they must develop their brain capacity through emotional security and empirical activity (play).

Regarding emotional security, the essential requirement is that there be one person, the mother (or mother substitute) with whom the infant can identify. Children raised in institutions, even those of the highest caliber, are mentally duller. Recognition of this fact has led to the use of foster homes rather than orphanages in many communities. Working mothers who leave their infants to the care of hired help could be handicapping their mental development. It is in this period that irrational fears and prejudices may become fixed.

It is with the third factor that we are here concerned as to the importance of toys. Babies begin to learn at birth. A beloved toy, usually a rag doll or stuffed animal or even

Illustration 56: Autoperipatetikos (walking doll) patented in England and the United States by Enoch Rice Morrison, in 1862. Has clock work mechanism for operating doll. Original box marked "Martin & Runyon, New York City." Lead mold for head is also shown. Doll stands 10in (25cm) tall; head mold is 3½in (9cm) high.

a favorite blanket, gives comfort and assurance to a small child. Even before taking his first steps into the outer world, he meets other people with more confidence if he has this familiar object clutched to him. For this self-chosen guardian, we suggest the name "Presence in the Crib" or "Social Weaning Toy." We can thus see that a properly selected crib toy can provide a strong secondary support to establishing emotional security.

Then finally there is the factor of empirical activity or play. Empirical simply means, derived from observation or experimentation. "Play is the child's work." And work at it he does, persistently and continually. At first his play is of the simplest nature: interlacing his fingers, fumbling at his toes, feeling the texture of his blanket, and watching dancing shadows. Next he loves a rattle to shake, beads to slide on a wire, a crib mobile to watch, a teething ring to chew on, or a pacifier.

The child wants to learn if you will let it. What we are most apt to overlook is the simplicity of the devices, the toys by which the child learns best. These things which stimulate his imagination and effectively serve his efforts to associate color, shape, sound, texture and the relation of cause and effect in his efforts to manipulate them are essential. At the Creative Playthings showroom in Princeton, New Jersey, it was a revelation to see the way in which the pre-school children turned to the simplest toys, those with abstract shapes suggesting the animal or human, the vehicle or building.

The observant mother often provides the right type of empirical activity unconsciously. An old trick of the busy housewife was to place the young one in a high-chair, smear his fingers with syrup and give him several feathers. He may spend an hour investigating this phenomenon of transferring these feathers from one sticky hand to the other. A collection of miscellaneous objects which we may call a "junk box" can be a more effective tool for our purpose than the latest fancy toy. Most toy manufacturers are free to admit that their toys are designed to appeal to the adult purchaser rather than for developing the creative and imaginative powers of the child. The contents of the "junk box" should be changed from time to time. New additions are quickly sorted out and tried in combinations with the old. It may consist of old spoons, spools, blocks, strings, crayons, bells, clothespins and other oddments.

This job of play is a tremendous one. The child has so much to learn that is basic; how to interrelate the myriad impressions that come through his senses — taste, smell, touch, sight and sound; how to coordinate them into actions which will bring satisfactions. His own imagination may provide a better guide to what is most useful to play with. Often one hears of an elaborate toy being pushed to one side while the child finds more fascination in playing with the packing case in which it came.

Here is an example as related by Joseph H. Peck in his common sense book *All about Men:* "When my sons were six and four, I bought them the best train I could find in a bargain basement. After playing with it for one day, they shoved it into a corner and there it stayed until their mother put it away. The following Christmas season, the younger boy wrote Santa, asking for a train he could push while doing his own huffing and tooting — and his own wrecking when he was so inclined.

"So don't expect your little son to gurgle with joy over the fancy toys you buy him. That replica of your new car is indeed beautiful, but he would prefer to receive four old baby buggy wheels and a few scraps of two-by-fours. From them he will construct a wagon, a wonderful vehicle whose wheels slant in different directions. Coming down the driveway, it looks like a fiddler crab uncertain just what direction to try next. He made it with his own hands, therefore it is beautiful, and his imagination will fit it with dreams not yet conceived by industrial engineers."

Illustration 57: "Le Garcon Comique," a paper toy with nodding heads and changeable paper hats. 19th century. 5in (13cm) tall.

LEFT: Illustration 58: Rocking Punch and Judy show with bells. A German paper toy dating in the late 19th century, 10in (25cm) by 7½in (18cm) by 3in (8cm).

Illustration 59: Sand toy depicting a dancing ballerina with musicians. Sand operated mechanism in back activates movement of doll. This is a paper toy made in Germany, c.1840. 10in (25cm) by 8in (18cm) by 2½in (6cm).

Illustration 60: "Circus International," a three-dimensional paper cut-out circus toy with French and German titles.

Chapter 10

The Church and the Child

OPPOSITE PAGE: Illustration 61: Saint
Michael with removable wax head, carved
wooden wings, arms and legs; elaborate
beadwork. Vienna, Austria. 18th century.
11in (28cm) tall.

To understand the culture of childhood, we must examine the artifacts of the child, especially the doll as we now know it. Our dolls have a distinguished heritage. We can trace them back to the early church when everyone in Europe was Catholic and the church was the patron of the arts. Any serious study of Europe leads us directly to the church. Our interest is in the religious figure the church used to present its teachings. The doll and the emerging child should be studied together in this period of early history.

Pilgrimages to the Holy Land had been undertaken by devout Christians in the 8th, 9th and 10th centuries. By the 10th and 11th centuries, it was believed that the end of the world was at hand, and that Jesus Christ would descend on Jerusalem and judge mankind. This religious revival in the 11th century heralded the start of the great Crusades. Peter the Hermit, a soldier who had become a monk, aroused widespread enthusiasm throughout Europe for these pilgrimages to Jerusalem. Military expeditions against the Muslims tried to take possession of Jerusalem and other places associated with the early life of Jesus. Relics such as the wood from the true cross, and the tears of Mary were brought back to the churches in Europe and sold to the faithful. The churches which had relics were visited by throngs of worshiping people. The abbots with an eye to trade, encouraged fairs to get started on their land. The Crusades were heavily promoted by the church, and younger sons of the nobility as well as whole families joined in this adventure. Many children were lost in these travels, but joined up with other children caught up in this madness. This children's crusade was the most amazing exploit by children in our early history.

The Crusades led to the opening of trade routes between the cultures of the East and West. This early commerce promoted the Chruch Fairs, and merchants from the East came with luxury goods for sale.

When Europe awakened from the Dark Ages, the monks had preserved many valuable records in their monasteries. The classics in Greek and Hebrew had been translated into Latin, the prevailing tongue, and stimulated new thoughts and ideas. This awakening or Renaissance began in the 14th century and a new age had arrived. Columbus discovered the new world, and the revival of learning was at hand. The invention of printing by Johann Gutenberg in 1439, and the printing of the famous Gutenberg Bible, spurred the learning process. In developing the printing press, he went into debt and lost everything he had. This delayed the immediate printing of books. Institutions of learning for both adults and children followed. The flowering of religious art and the rise of the humanities began. Our study of dolls and child development is part of this emergence of the humanities. One of the world's great artists Albrecht Dürer (1471-1528) appeared on the scene. He represented the true Renaissance man and left us a great deal that reflects himself in this time period. He used the artist model to help him paint the human form. His medium ranged the whole scope of art: woodcuts, engravings, drawings, sculpture and paintings. He was active in the humanist movement and was an admirer of Martin Luther. His work "Praying Hands" is famous today as an expression of religious feeling.

Christianity flourished in Europe and the church was its representative. Many great cathedrals had been built throughout Europe. They took many generations to complete, but were continually used during the process. They were, of course, monastic buildings, the monks designing and taking care of the chancel, the cloisters, the library and offices. The people, led by the aristocratic land owners, controlled the nave, and this huge space was suitable for both feast and fun days as well as for religious purposes. The sacred area surrounding the altar was enriched with religious art. The church became the richest landholder and was more powerful than the state in many areas, a situation that was bound to cause conflict.

The accepted date for Christ's birth marks our beginning of time, or Anno Domini on our calendar. The tremendous influence of the story of the Holy Family has given special meaning to the world, although scholars still have not found the historic Jesus. The nativity story as told in the beautiful King James version of the *Bible* has influenced our culture to understand the wonder and beauty of the new born babe, and the protection and care both mother and child need from the father. This story has inspired artists to create the scene we know as the creche.

OPPOSITE PAGE: Illustration 62: Holy family creche figures. *Mary* 15in (38cm), *Joseph* 19in (48cm), *Jesus* 5in (13cm) in height. Italy. 18th century.

Illusrtration 63: Three wooden religious figures, 27in (69cm), 20in (51cm) and 13½in (34cm) tall. Tallest figure is dressed in later period costume. Churches redressed their saints in the latest fashions, confusing them with fashion dolls. Probably Germany. Late 18th century.

The earliest creche was a living one, conceived by St. Francis of Assisi. In 1223, the pope gave him permission to recreate the Bethlehem story in the church at Grecia, Italy, near Assisi, on Christmas eve. A manger was filled with hay, and the figures were real, including the animals. The towns people came in with lighted tapers and torches. "St. Francis sang the gospel and the people listened with joy and wonder." This was reported by Alice K. Early in her book *English Dolls and Puppets.* Our 1951 trip included a visit to this pastoral area.

The artists creche started with only the Holy Family (Illustration 62 and color photo on page 34) and enlarged finally to include not only the animals, but the heavenly host and the awed towns people as well. The creche reached its zenith in Naples, Italy, around the 18th century. The bodies of the figures were made of tow and wire, and could bend. The heads and shoulders were moulded in terra cotta, and their clothing was typical of the period. The creche exhibited at New York City's Metropolitan Museum of Art each Christmas season has a large tree decorated with angels and cherubs. At the base

of the tree is the ruins of a Roman temple. Little houses that surround a village square show figures of the traditional scene — the Holy Family, the shepherds, the Magi and oriental Moors.

From ths time foreward the toy creche became a classic Christmas pleasure for children. In Catholic countries, toys for little children were often oriented towards their religion. Toy chapels to teach the sequence of the mass, dolls representing patron saints, the Christmas Christ Child, even monks and nuns and church dignitaries in their typical habits and costumes are still popular toys in some parts of the world.

Our visit to the Munich National Museum in 1951 gave us our first understanding of the dramatic power of the creche, or krippe. The many scenes contain over 6000 figures. Although many fine examples of children's playthings did not survive the bombings of World War II, the creche figures on display in the basement remained in tact. This is the largest such collection in the world.

Noah's Ark

Many toys were influenced by religious figures, artifacts and Bible stories. One of the most important treasures in our collection is our Noah's Ark. Our illuminated *Naples Bible* is a copy of a 14th century Old Testament manuscript which tells the story of the building of the Ark, the flood, and of Noah's sacrifice. The Ark was built of resinous woods and reeds soaked in pitch, according to Jehovah's instructions. Then came the rains for forty days and nights, and the Ark with Noah's family and two of each animal, floated over the immensity of the resulting desolation.

In 1983, The Philadelphia Maritime Museum had a special holiday exhibit called "Two by Two, Animals and Arks in Toyland." Pasted beneath one of the opening roofs of a toy ark was this poem:

> *God saw men's wicked ways*
> *And nipped them in the bud,*
> *He let it rain for forty days*
> *And drowned them with the flood.*
> *The bad all died, but mark!*
> *God saved good Noah's life.*
> *He saved him in a mighty Ark*
> *With his three sons and wife.*
> *And two of every kind*
> *Of insect, beast and bird -*

Noah's Arks have been popular playthings for many years. They apparently originated in the Oberammergau region of Germany in the mid 17th century. Animals carved for creche scenes could be interchanged to interpret other *Bible* stories such as Noah's Ark. These arks were also produced in Berchtesgaden, Erzgebirge, and Sonneberg, Germany, as well as Oberammergau, and started as a cottage industry. Later this became a guild industry and eventually they were massed produced. These arks were commonly known as "box toys" as the family and animals were stored in the ark with a hinged roof which was used as a box. These arks were usually designed with a porch, and often with a dove and an olive branch painted on the roof.

In the Middle Ages, the story of the flood was a familiar one. It was one of the popular subjects of mystery plays, and puppet shows which included Punch and Judy.

The ark pictured from our collection is dated around 1840. It has been played with by many children, so some of the animals are missing or broken. But still it makes an impressive procession when set up. The interest in this toy by children lasted longer than most — from the mid 14th century to the mid 19th century. Its religious nature made it acceptable for Sunday play. It's variety of animals would delight the interest and imagination of any child, in solitary play or with family and friends.

In the American Colonies, the Germans in Pennsylvania whittled arks and animals. And in the 1930s, both Sears, Roebuck and Montgomery Ward carried these toys in their catalogues. Rarely has a theme toy lasted so long.

The earliest years of the church met with persecution, and not until Charlemagne (768-814) was converted did it begin to prosper. The church used every means possible to help the illiterate learn of Christ and the stories of the Bible. By the 10th century, church art thrived. Carved religious figures representing the Holy Family, saints, angels, and so forth, were in demand by all the churches in Europe, and the wood carvers thrived. Unfortunately, most of those figures that survived are from the 17th and

Illustration 64: Wooden saint (possibly representing the apostle Matthew) giving a blessing. European. 15in (38cm) tall.

18th centuries. The artist model with articulated ball jointed arms and legs were expertly made. Religious figures become a part of our doll story. We find that some of these religious figures had been redressed in the costume of the day, and mistakenly considered Fashion Dolls.

Church figure and artist's mannequin makers were crafts people with a long history, and they inherited and developed skills of high order. It was surely they who were commissioned to make the first dolls, splendid creatures, intended for children of aristocrats, and often presented as tokens of political prestige, rather than from an affection and understanding of the child. In the dolls that survived to us from the late 17th century and before, we can see clearly the connection between the religious figure and the doll.

To understand our early dolls it is essential to realize the sharp distinction that existed between the aristocracy and the rest of humanity. Until the Industrial Revolution began to show its effects at the end of the 18th century, the world belonged to the landed gentry, and most of the dolls that we find from those early days belonged to their daughters.

And what of the thousands of less fortunate children? What were their pleasures, their playthings? Our information and evidence is very scant, but we can find some of the answers if we turn our attention to the traditional fairs.

Originally pagan festivals, the great fairs that were held on saints days throughout Europe from the Middle Ages even until today, were for peasants, farmers and lower classes, the only festivity and excitement in their drab and hard working existances. Originally a curious mixture of piety and commerce, the fairs became important centers for trade, with merchandise brought from far off countries. Thorold Rodgers, has a description of the Sturbridge Fair, the greatest of all English fairs, that could hardly be bettered.

"The Venetian and Genoese merchant came with his precious stock, his Italian silks and velvet, his delicate glass. The Flemish weaver was present with his linen, the Spaniard with his stock of iron, the Norwegian with his tar and pitch. The Hanse towns sent furs and amber, and precious stones from the East were supplied through the markets of Moscow and Novgordod." There was tin from

Cornwell, lead from Derbyshire, and of course the woolpacks that were the most precious of all.

As the centuries went by and the focus of religion changed, the fairs became more secular and more rowdy. Describing the famous Bartholemew Fair of London in his book *English Fairs and Markets*, William Addison says: "Every component of a fair was there from the beginning, every manifestation and expression of its piety, its feasting, its greed, its folly — and all, it seems, in melodramatic proportions. We have the rabble of sick and diseased gabbling their prayers at the altar, the chapmen haggling in the porch, peddlers crying their wares and chaffering in the churchyard, minstrels, mummers, and acrobats, with clerks and friars going among them to beg alms, all to the accompaniment of the lowing of oxen, the neighing of horses and the bleating of sheep."

Catering to the meager pockets of the common people who might have pennies to spend, perhaps only this one time in the whole year, there were many stalls and pedlars at the fair who catered to these poorer patrons with tawdry gimcrack wares. The very word "tawdry" originated at St. Audrey's Fair, held in Ely, England, since the time of Henry I in honor of St. Etheldreda, popularly known as St. Audrey.

Among these cheap, tinselly wares we know that there were toys for children. The simple dolls that were bought at the fairs, which by the 18th century were collectively known as "Bartholemew Babies," were for many little girls the only dolls they would ever own. Since they were as flimsy as today's carnival Kewpie dolls, none have survived to us, as far as we know.

London Exposition

One more fair of particular interest to doll collectors happened in London in 1851 and was referred to as the Great Exhibition. It resembled our current World's Fairs that take place now every four or five years in different countries of the world. Merchants from all over the globe participated in this huge effort.

England was in transition from the world of farming and handcrafts to the mechanization of the Industrial Revolution. Queen Victoria was on the throne, and her consort Prince Albert assumed the task of sponsoring this fair. From the book *London 1851, The Year of the Great*

Illustration 65: Noah's Ark made for Rayleys of London, England, by Austrian peasants. Purchased at Marshall Fields in Chicago, Illinois, in 1940. 13½in (34cm) by 10in (25cm) by 10in (25cm).

Exhibition, by Eric de Mare, we get a remarkable overview of this monumental project. A royal commission of 27 members was set up, headed by Prince Albert, and Gladstone was among its members.

William Culbitt, architect and chairman of the building committee had been working on a large glass building for a greenhouse on a big estate. It occurred to him that this concept, enlarged many fold to include huge trees, shrubs and flowers in Hyde Park, might be an answer to the necessary structure. When presented to the building commission, of which he was chairman, this idea was accepted, and thus was born the Crystal Palace. The Royal Commission divided the inside space into many booths and arcades, alloting these areas equally to England, her colonies, and to foreign countries. This fair was truly international.

On a rainy May first, at eleven o'clock, half a million people gathered to witness the opening ceremonies. Flags of all nations flew along the gleaming roof. With all the pagentry associated with the throne, the Royal Family entered the Crystal Palace, followed by the Prince of Wales in Highland dress, and the princess in white lace with a wreath of wild roses in her hair. Trumpets sounded, cannons boomed, and the 1851 Great Exhibition opened in style.

Of particular interest to the doll world were two men, Montanari and Pierotti, who came to this fair to show their new technique in doll making. Their dolls were made of wax. Hair was inserted into their heads, brows and lashes with a hot needle, a strand at a time. Flesh tones were exceptionally beautiful, and these dolls were elegantly dressed and wonderfully displayed in group settings with antique furniture and appropriate acces-

sories. Naturally, these dolls were expensive, far above the reach of the average child; yet with the advent of a growing, successful middle-class, and the landed gentry, they were very popular. For the small child or baby, an adjacent case showed a variety of cheap rag dolls.

The great success of this fair, and the overwhelming crowds that arrived in London, sorely taxed the available housing. Caught up in the excitement of the time, local citizens shared their homes with many of the foreign visitors. It was as if London had entered a new era, and a new doll was part of this experience.

In all the great Calendar of Saints Days, the most important for children was St. Nicholas Day, December 6th. This early Christian Bishop, with his legendary miracles, had become the children's own Saint, and the presents they received to honor his feast were the origin of our own Christmas gift giving. For good children, there was gingerbread stamped with the image of the saint; for little boys a toy horse, perhaps; for their sisters, most likely a swaddled baby doll, to remind her of the coming of the baby King of Heaven. Many such swaddled baby dolls are to be found in collections today, unrecognized, and perhaps unvalued by their owners.

In our travels, as we searched for the antecendents of the wooden, wax and papier-mâché dolls, we acquired a number of fine church figures, swaddled babies, and even ancient artists mannequins. Some of them are works of art of great beauty and sophistication. Others, no less beautiful, are primitive and touching in their naive expressions of faith. They hold among them the clues to the origins of the dolls so beloved by the children of the 19th century, so prized by the doll collectors of today.

Illustration 66: Two wooden swaddling dolls. The larger doll, 9in (23cm) tall, was made in Bohemia in the late 18th century. The smaller doll, 5in (13cm) tall, was made in Oberamagau, Germany, in the late 19th century; the head is rotated by turning the rod at the base of the doll.

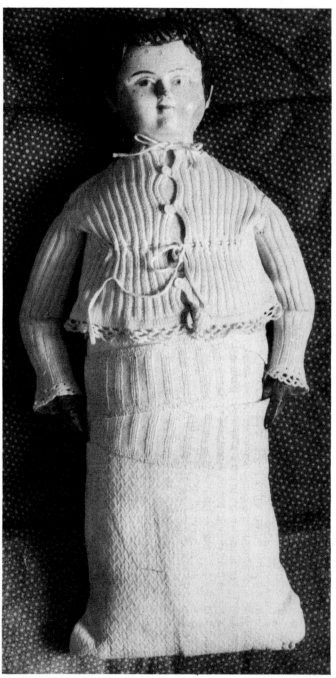

Illustration 67: Swaddling doll with deep-chested shoulder head, bag body and leather arms. Hand-knit sweater. All original. 20in (51cm) tall. Germany. Early 19th century. Later versions have been seen with china heads.

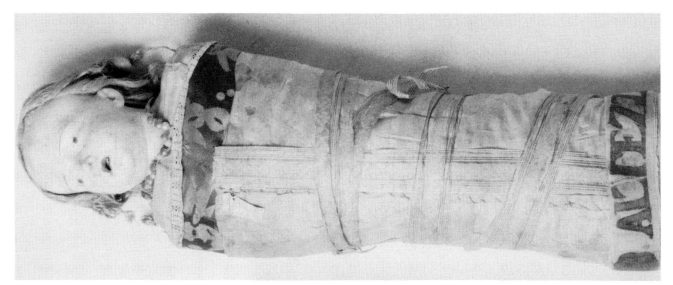

Illustration 68: Papier-mâché swaddling from the Shrine of Our Lady of DiLoreto, Italy, wrapped in red silk and wearing beads. He has a sorrowful expression on his face and has flax hair. 20in (51cm) tall.

BELOW: *Illustration 69*: Pressed tin votive figures generally purchased in church gift shops. c.1890. 5 to 8in (13 to 22cm) tall.

Chapter 11

Museums and the Artifacts of Childhood

As we have pursued the hobby of collecting dolls and expanded it to include the broader area of playthings, we have visited many of the great museums of this country. In reviewing our findings, we are amazed that museums have paid so little attention to the world of the child. In fact if it were not for the inclusion of paintings of children in the department of visual arts, or an occasional small chair or cradle in a collection of furniture, or a child's spoon or mug in the work of a noted silversmith, most museums might suggest that we came into this world fully grown.

Let us note typical examples of this blind spot. The Metropolitan Museum of Art in New York City has established a remarkably fine youth's section with exhibits and library designed to introduce young folks to the visual arts. (Indeed, we observed many adults were visiting it to get their basis for art appreciation.) We found that their youth's library had no books on toys or dolls. The librarian explained it was their policy to include only books relating to material in their collections. She was somewhat amazed to hear from us that there was an extraordinarily fine 18th century English wooden doll in the American wing and a group of toys in a Pennsylvania German exhibit. In a sense though, she was quite right. The doll was there as a bit of room decor. The toys were there as illustrations of the artwork of a culture. Neither was there representing the world of the child.

In the Boston Museum of Fine Arts, there are also two very fine 18th century English wooden dolls. They are kept in storage in the textile department because of the materials in which they are dressed. Anyone interested in them as dolls must make special arrangements to see them.

Historical museums are more apt to include toys and dolls which were associated with some notable person or event — such as a rag doll made by Mrs. Alexander Hamilton, or the doll which was used to smuggle medicines during the Civil War, or the first doll brought to the West Coast by wagon train. When we asked at the main desk of the Chicago Field Museum where to look for toys in their displays, we were told that there were none. Yet we found about ten included for this associative reason. On the other hand, the Museum of the City of New York, the select repository of artifacts from the attics of many old New York families, has assembled a

large group of toys and dolls and is giving specialized attention to them. Their many displays are imaginative and would delight both children and adults, thanks to John Darcy Noble's sensitive and artistic treatment.

In recent years there are other signs that the child is being recognized by the museums as part of the human race. The Department of Cultural History of the Smithsonian Institution is displaying our cultural background, not in the old fashion of putting all ceramics in one place, all the carpenter's tools in another, all the toys in rows on shelves, and so on, but in natural settings representative of the living customs of the era. In these settings one now sees a doll here, some toy dishes there, or marbles where a child may have left them. We believe that for many reasons it is of mutual advantage for museums and doll collectors to work together.

Children's museums (including special departments of more general museums as in the American Museum of Natural History) are devoted to the activities of school age children. These include natural history hobbies, arts and crafts, games, planetariums, and collections of dolls and playthings from our own past or from foreign lands, to broaden the child's vision and arouse his imagination. These museums cooperate closely with the schools or may be part of the school system, as in Detroit, Michigan. Material is prepared for circulation to classrooms, and classes make guided tours to the museum's exhibit halls. Parents may also learn much from them, but they are directed primarily to the interests of the school child.

Another innovation in museums that has intrigued us is The Museum of Childhood in Edinburgh, Scotland. This is a museum designed for the adult to learn about childhood. The artifacts assembled there include not only playthings but anything particularly related to the life of the child. At its inception, the curator roamed the streets and back alleys of Edinburgh, looking for poor children with whom to swap new dolls for their homemade raggedy substitutes. He showed real ingenuity in collecting the true artifacts of childhood in his area. We know that this is a very popular museum.

This basic thought, that a museum (or a specialized department therein) be directed to the education of the adult regarding the important factors in the life of the child, has brought to our minds some new and challenging questions. The principal one is: How can museums develop the displays relating to those years of the child's life where the artifacts are few in number and extremely simple in character, yet essential to the most important growth years — the pre-school years. The importance of play in the early years is discussed in more detail elsewhere in this book.

As laymen, visiting museums together for the past sixty plus years, we have been impressed with the progressive change in outlook of museum practices. They have become socialized. Instead of dreary rows of cases jammed with artifacts, we now have exciting scenes of regional habitats in natural history; working models in science and technology; dioramas of history; and so on. The comfort of the visitor is well considered, and explanatory material freely available; both printed and oral, from tapes. All this has vastly improved communication with the public — illiterate or learned, laymen or specialists, the casual visitor, the teacher, the parent or potential parent, the social worker, the service clubs, the ethical leaders, all can draw inspiration firmly rooted in organized knowledge.

At the same time, behind the scenes, there will still be the need for the systemized collection of artifacts from the past and from varied cultures, relating to the world of childhood. These provide the research worker in the social sciences with the means for elucidating general principles; principles which can enable mankind to attain his potential.

The Children's Museum in Indianapolis, Indiana, is probably the most complete museum for children of all ages anywhere. It is remarkably well balanced, displays are first rate, and it is always a beehive of childhood activity. The Caplan Collection (Creative Playthings) has been donated here.

There is growing evidence as to the importance of the pre-school years in the life of man. We would like to suggest that the museums accept the challenge of communicating the significance and importance of these findings to the public in three major aspects. These are emotional security, good nutrition and empirical activity. That they further recognize the value to be derived from the collection and study of the artifacts relating to the children from birth through adolescence. In such a study, we would expect that playthings will rank high.

Our dream for an International Museum of Childhood — some Guidelines.

A Museum of Childhood should have as its first objective the education of adults and parents concerning childhood development. This would not preclude the inclusion of a Child's Gallery where adults could observe what interests children. This activity room could be a part of the research program.

This Museum could be developed to include two major junctional lines. First, a collection of artifacts of the past — toys, clothing, furniture and so forth, particularly designed for the child. This should include the major cultures of the world, drawing heavily on the folk arts of these cultures. This would be a major attraction for visitors, and provide research material for students of child development. Toy designers might find this a good source for ideas. These displays could demonstrate the way in which certain artifacts changed to meet the changing social and technological developments over a period of time. Finally, these artifacts of the past could be supplemented by displays demonstrating what current research shows to be important in the development of the child from conception to puberty.

The Museum staff should include several disciplines: an administrator, a curator with a sound background in the arts and children, a librarian, an educational consultant, and a pediatric consultant.

Such an institution could flourish in conjunction with several locals. It could be a part of a museum complex such as the Smithsonian, the Metropolitan, the Carnegie, the Los Angeles County Museum or several others we could mention. It might be a project of UNICEF as an adjunct to the United Nations. Or a University campus might be the logical setting, for example Teacher's College at Columbia University in New York City. Possibly the University of California at San Diego, which has developed several new colleges and is closely associated with the Salk Institute (concerned with Life Sciences), might fill this role. We need a place to go to study the whole child.

Other Dolls in the Mathes Collection

Illustration 71: Russian tea cozy doll with papier-mâché head and hands. 19th century. 13in (33cm) tall.

Illustration 72: Large Russian tea cozy doll. 19th century. 18in (46cm) tall.

Illustration 73: Left to right: China head doll with blue eyes. c.1870. 12½in (32cm) tall. China head doll with blue eyes. c.1850. 16in (41cm) tall. China head doll with brown eyes (which were exceptional). c.1850. 15in (38cm) tall. All are wearing homemade clothing.

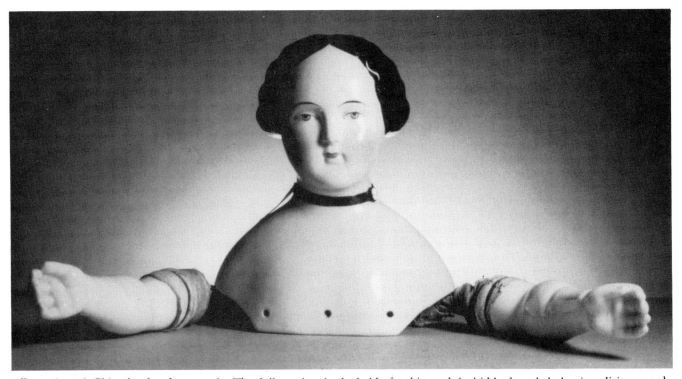

Illustration 74: China head and arms only. The doll was lost in the hold of a ship, and the kid body and clothes just disintegrated. Germany. c.1840. Head 8in (20cm) high.

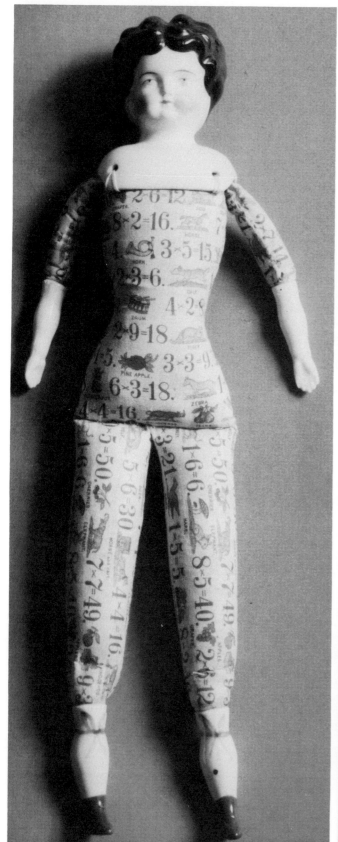

OPPOSITE PAGE: Illustration 77: Nymphenburg porcelain doll with cage body and wearing all original clothes. 14in (36cm) tall.

Illustration 75: China doll with cloth body printed with multiplication tables. Germany. Late 19th century. 16in (41cm) tall.

Illustration 76: Columbia rag doll. 20th century. American. 15in (38cm) tall.

Illustration 78: Angel candleholders from Berchtesgaden, Germany. Early 20th century. 22in (56cm) tall.

OPPOSITE PAGE: Illustration 80: Four coiffured papier-mâché head dolls. Gold dress. 1840. 21in (53cm) tall. Munich doll with kid body, wooden arms and legs, wearing a black silk dress. 20in (51cm) tall. Munich doll with kid body, wooden arms and legs, wearing a printed cotton dress. c.1830. 16in (41cm) tall. Doll wearing pink gauze store bought dress has a cloth body with kid arms and is 14½in (37cm) tall.

Illustration 79: Two wax swaddling dolls, 14in (36cm) and 15in (38cm) tall. Both church figures representing the Christ Child. Probably Italy. 18th century.

Illustration 81: Lillian Smith reproduction of a doll head from an old mold, wearing 1830s hair style. (Mold shown with doll head.) 1950s. 17½in (45cm) tall.

OPPOSITE PAGE: Illustration 83: Doll labelled "Superior 2015." Papier-mâché head; leather arms; appropriate old clothes. Germany. c.1860.

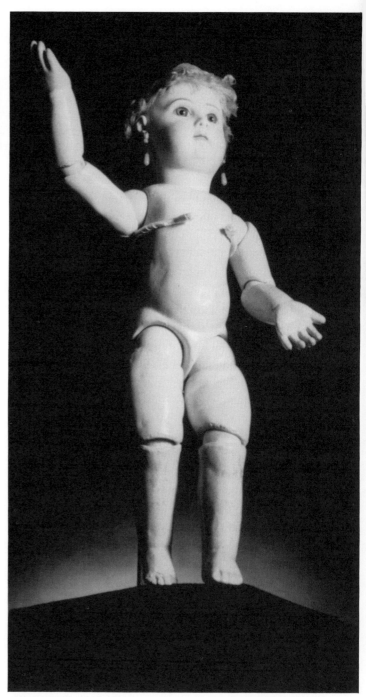

Illustration 82: Emile Jumeau bisque-headed doll with composition body. France. Mid 19th century. *Ex-collection Imogene Anderson.*

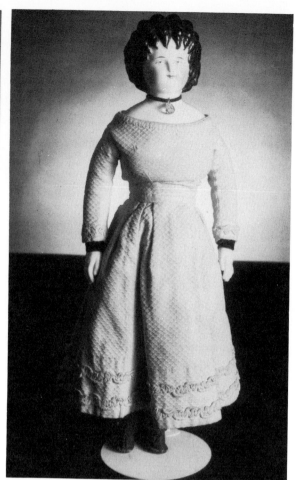

CLOCKWISE: Illustration 84: Porcelain doll, all original. Germany. 1860s. 22½in (57cm) tall.

Illustration 85: China head doll with cloth body, china hands and leather shoes. All original. Germany. c1870s. 17in (43cm) tall.

Illustration 86: Lenci felt doll with molded face. Italy. 17in (43cm) tall.

Illustration 87: Leather-faced nurse doll (left) has nursing tools in an inner pocket tied around her waist. England. 18th century. 9in (23cm) tall. Folk doll made from a forked twig is all original. America. 1830. 12½in (32cm) tall.

RIGHT: Illustration 88: Simon & Halbig bisque-headed doll with composition body. All original. Germany. Early 20th century. 22in (56cm).

Exhibitions of the Mathes Collection

COLLEGES: CALIFORNIA
    California State University at Northridge
    Long Beach State University
    Pierce Junior College
    Palomar Community College

MUSEUMS:
    Long Beach Museum of Art, California
    San Diego Museum of Art, California
    deYoung Museum, San Francisco, California
    Abby Aldrich Rockefeller Folk Art Museum - Williamsburg, Virginia
    Mingei International Museum of World Folk Art — San Diego, California
    Mathes Community Cultural Center - Escondido, California

LIBRARIES:
    San Diego City Library, California
    Carlsbad City Library, California
    Escondido Public Library, California

Illustration 89: Bronze portrait heads of Ruth E. Mathes (1892-) and Robert C. Mathes (1891-1985), by Ira Chaffin, sculptor. Unveiled at the Mathes Community Cultural Center, Escondido, California, December 16th, 1983. Donated by Robert Harris Mathes and Joyce Mathes Malcolm.

Bibliography 1:

The Child Emerges

Early Childrens Books. Pierpont Morgans Library, New York City. David R. Godine, Publisher, Boston. Copyright 1975.

Little Wide — Awake, an anthology from Victorian childrens books and periodicals by Ann and Fernand G. Renier, selected by Leonard de Vries.

English Fairs and Markets, by William Addison, Illustrated by Barbara Jones. Published by R. T. Botsford Ltd, London 1953.

The Story of the Wisemen, as told by St. Matthew. Carvings by Gislebertus, text by Regine Pernoud and Canon Grivot. Story of the role of the Cathedral in the life of the Middle Ages. Copyright 1964 by Trianon Press, Canada by Holt, Rinehart and Winston. First edition.

Miniature Travelers, by Amy Thomas Golding. Publisher, Marshall Jones Co. Francestown, NH. 1956.

Notre Dame of Paris, by Allan Temko. 1952. Time Inc. Book Division.

The Story of King Arthur and His Knights, by Howard Pyle. Dover Press. 1965. First published by Charles Scribners' Sons in 1903.

The Power of Play, by Frank and Theresa Caplan. 1974. Anchor Press/Doubleday, Garden City, NY. Founders of Creative Playthings.

From Forgotten Children's Books. Dover Publications Inc., New York City. 1969. Dover Pictorial Archive Series.

The Human Side of History — Mans' Manners and Morals and Games, by Raymond Friday Licke. Hawthorn Books Inc. New York City.

Child Life in New England 1790-1840. A 27-page booklet, Sturbridge, MA. 1966. Editor, Catherine Finneley. 2nd printing.

Childs Life in Colonial Days, by Alice Morse Earle. 1899. Publisher, The Macmillian Company. Second printing, 1966.

Colonial Virginians at Play, by Jane Carson. Colonial Williamsburg Publications. 1965. Distributed by the University of Virginia Press, Charlottesville, VA.

Dolls the Wide World Over, by Manfred Buchmann and Claus Hansmann. Crown Publishers, Inc. New York. Collaboration with Patrick Murray, Museum of Childhood, Edinburgh, Scotland. English translation from German in 1973.

Games and Pastimes of Childhood, by Jacques Stella. 1657. Engraved by Claudine B. Stella. Published by Dover Press Archives, New York City.

Songs of Innocence, by William Blake. 1789. Dover Press Publications, New York City. 1971.

Bibliography 2:

Toys and Dolls

Children's Toys of Bygone Days, by Karl Grober. English version by Philip Hereford. Publisher, Frederick A. Stokes Co. 1928.

Dolls and Puppets, by Max von Boehn. English version by Josephine Nicoll. Publisher, David McKay Co., New York City.

Album of American History, colonial period. Editor, James Truslow Adams. Publisher, Charles Scribners, Sons. 1944.

Wonderland of Work, by Clara L. Mateau. New and revised editions with additions by Joshua Rose. Publisher, Cassell and Co. Limited. New York, London and Paris. 1884.

Extraordinary Popular Delusions and the Madness of Crowds, by Charles Mackay, Ltd, with foreward by Bernard Baruch. Publisher, L. C. Page and Co., Boston. 1852.

London 1851 — The Year of the Great Exhibition, by Erc de Mare. The Folio Society. London 1972. Lithography throughout.

Queen Victoria's Sketchbook, by Marina Warner. Crown Publishers Inc. New York. 1979.

Pollock's Dictionary of English Dolls, Mary Hillier, editor. Copyright 1982 by Pollocks Toy Museum. Crown Publishers Inc. New York City.

Decline and Fall of the Wooden Doll, by Ruth E. and R. C. Mathes. Reprint from the 1964 *Doll Collectors Manual.*

Research Applied to Dolls, by Ruth E. and Robert C. Mathes. Reprint from 1973 *Doll Collectors Manual.*

Modes and Manners, by Max von Boehn in four volumes. Scholarly treatment of the social history of the 15th, 16th, 17th and 18th centuries in Europe. English translation by Joan Joshua. 1932-1935. Publisher, George G. Harrap and Co., Ltd. London, Bombay and Sydney.

Queen Victoria's Dolls, by Frances H. Low. Illustrated by Alan Wright. Publisher, George Newner, Limited, London. 1894.

The Atlas of Medieval Man, Culture of the 11th through 15th Centuries. Slybil Strother, editor. Publisher, St. Martins Press, Inc., New York City. 1979.

The Doll Book, by Laura B. Starr. Publisher, The Outing Publishing Co., New York City. 1908.

Homo Ludens — A Study of Play — Element in Culture, by J. Huizmga. Publisher, The Beacon Press, Boston. 1955.

The Inquisition of the Middle Ages, by Henry Charles Lea, with abridgment by Margaret Nicholson. Publisher, Macmillan and Co., New York City. 1961.

Fashion the Mirror of History, A Chanticleer Press Edition by Michael and Ariane Batterterry, Greenwich House. Distributed by Crown Publishers Inc. New York City. 1982.

Dolls, by Esther Singleton. Published by Payson and Clarke, Ltd. New York City. 1927.

Childrens' Toys of Yesterday. Special winter number of *The Studio,* edited by C. Goffrey Holmes. 1932.

Toys of Other Days, by Mrs. F. Nevill Jackson. The Country Life Library, published by Country Life Ltd. and Charles Scribner's Sons, New York City. MCMVIII.

The Fascinating Story of Dolls (1941), *More About Dolls* (1946), *Still More About Dolls* (1950), *Your Dolls and Mine* (1952) all by Janet Pagter Johl. Publisher, H. L. Lindquest New York City.

English Dolls, Effigies and Puppets, by Alice K. Early. Publisher, B. T. Balsford Ltd., London. 1955.

Dolls, A Guide for Collectors, by Clara Hollard Fawcett. Publisher, H. L. Lindquist, New York City. 1947.

A Book of Dolls, by Gwen White. Publisher, The Macmillan Company, New York. 1956.

Dolls of the World, by Gwen White. Publisher, Charles T. Branford Company, Massachusetts. 1962.

European and American Dolls, by Gwen White. Publisher, G. P. Putnam's Sons. 1966.

Dolls of Yesterday, by Eleanor St. George. Publisher, Charles Scribner's Sons. New York and London. 1948.

Pageant of Toys, by Mary Hillier. Publisher, Taplinger Publishing Company, Inc., New York City. 1966.

Wonderful Dolls of Wax, by Elizabeth Gerken. Printed by Calico Print Shop, Wichita, Kansas. 1964.

Wonderful Dolls of Papier Mâché, by Elizabeth Gerken. Published by Doll Research Association, Box 6012, College Press Station, Lincoln, Nebraska, 68506. 1970.

The Fabulous Dollhouse of the Twenties, by John Darcy Noble, Dover Publications, New York. 1976.

A Treasury of Beautiful Dolls, by John Darcy Noble. Published by Hawthorne Books. MCMLXXI.

Dolls, by John Darcy Noble. Publisher, Walker & Company, New York. 1967.

The Collectors Encyclopedia of Dolls, by Dorothy S., Elizabeth A. and Evelyn J. Coleman. Crown Publishers Inc. New York. 1968.

The Collector's Book of Doll Clothes, by Dorothy S., Elizabeth A. and Evelyn J. Coleman. Crown Publishers, Inc., New York. 1975.

Lenci Dolls, by Dorothy S. Coleman. Publisher, Hobby House Press, Maryland.

American Folk Dolls, by Wendy Lavitt. Publisher, Alfred A. Knopf, New York. 1982.

The Art of Dolls, by Madeline Osborne Merrill. Edited by Estelle Johnston. Publisher, Hobby House Press, Inc., Maryland. 1985.

Dolls and Toys of the Essex Institute, by Madeline and Richard Merrill. Printed by Woodland Publishing Company.

Chinas, by Mona Borger. Printed by A. R. Lithographers, Hayword, California. 1983.

German Doll Encyclopedia 1800-1939, by Jürgen and Marianne Cieslik. English Edition published by Hobby House Press, Inc., Maryland. 1985.

An Illustrated History of Toys, by Karl Ewald Fritzsch and Manfred Bachmann. English translation by Ruth Michaelis-Jena. Abbey Library, London. 1966.

History of Toys, by Antonia Fraser. Printed in Germany by K. G. Lohse. Delacorte Press. 1966.

The World of Toys, by Robert Culff. The Hamlyn Publishing Company, Limited, London, New York. 1969. Printed in Italy by Arnoldo Mondadori, Editor.

Folk Toys, by Emanuel Hercikl. Prague, Czechoslavakia. 1952.

Doll Houses in America, by Flora Gill Jacobs. Publisher, Charles Scribner's Sons. New York. 1974.

History of Doll Houses, by Flora Gill Jacobs. Publisher, Charles Scribner's Sons. New York. 1953.

and Doll Houses, by Flora Gill Jacobs and Estrid Faurholt. Publisher, Charles E. Tuttle Company, land, Vermont - Tokyo, Japan. 1967.

Doll Houses, by Vivien Greene. Publisher, B. T. ...rd Ltd., London. 1955.

Doll Houses, by Cathrine Dorris Callicott and Holderness. Story of a personal collection. ..., William Morrow and Company, Inc. ...k. 1978.

...que Furniture, by Herbert F. and Peter B. Schiffer. Livingston Publishing Co. Pennsylvania. 1972. (The Chester County Historical Society and Museum have an old doll house that reflects 19th century Philadelphia history.)

A Study of Dolls, by G. Stanley Hall and A. Caswell Ellis. A 69-page booklet dated 1897. Copyrights by E. L. Kelogg and Company, New York.

Fashion Plates 1770-1899, by Vyvyan Holland. Publisher, B. T. Botsford, Ltd., London. 1955.

Fashions in Paris 1797-1897, by Octave Uzanne. London: William Heinemann. New York: Charles Scribners and Sons. MDCCCXCVIII. Translated from the French by Lady Mary Loyd. (250 hand colored plates.)

Dolls and Doll-makers, by Mary Hillier. Published by G. P. Putnam's Sons, New York. 1968.

The History of Wax Dolls, by Mary Hillier. Published by Hobby House Press, Inc. Maryland. 1985.

London 1851, by Eric de Mare. Folio Society, London. 1872.

Unique and Interesting Antique Dolls, by Pegby. Limited Edition, privately published in Sussex, England. Recent edition, no date.

Quarterly of New York State Historical Association, Early American Dolls, by E. P. Anderson. July 1937.

The Illuminated Naples Bible, by Gabriel Bise. Crescent Books by Crown Publishers, Inc. New York City.

Mister Andrews' School - 1837-1842, The Students' Journal Transcribed and Illustrated by Ellen Swartzlander. Bucks County Historical Society. Livingston Publishing Company, Narberth, Pennsylvania, 1958.

Auction Catalogue: Richard W. Withington, Inc. Doll collection of Barbara Rose and others. October 30-31, 1980.

Auction Catalogue: Richard W. Withington, Inc. Gladyse H. Hilsdorf doll collection, page 1. September 20-21, 1985.

Almost any auction catalogue from a reputable auction house.

(We have included a long list of books, divided into two subjects. *The Child Emerges* - it is essential to search through the books that belong to the humanities, of which we are a part.

Books About Dolls - some of these books have misinformation, and we all make mistakes. It is the doll that must speak to us. A few dolls have come to us from the 18th century, but most that are available are from the 19th and 20th centuries. The 19th century is known as the Golden Age of Dolls. The Colemans have become the tabulators and geneologists for the doll world. We suggest that you add their books to your library, especially *The Collectors Encyclopedia of Dolls,* Volume 1.)

Index